THE POMEGRANATE BUSKER

A Travel Adventure in Search of New Zealand Rock Stardom

In memory of Jazz, the best farm dog that ever lived.

Copyright

The Pomegranate Busker:
A Travel Adventure in Search of New Zealand Rock Stardom

ISBN: 978-0-6451187-3-5
Imprint: Simon Michael Prior
10 9 8 7 6 5 4 3 2 1

Copyright © 2022 by Simon Michael Prior

All rights reserved. No part of this book may be reproduced or transmitted in any form or by any means without written permission from the author.

CONTENTS

1. THE ONE AND ONLY 5
2. TAKE A CHANCE ON ME 6
3. THE KING OF WISHFUL THINKING 17
4. CENTERFOLD 26
5. IN THE AIR TONIGHT 33
6. WHEN WILL I BE FAMOUS? 40
7. BLAME IT ON THE BOOGIE 42
8. THE POMEGRANATE BUSKER 50
9. THINGS CAN ONLY GET BETTER 61
10. IT'S MY PARTY 67
11. I STILL HAVEN'T FOUND WHAT I'M LOOKING FOR 76
12. DANGER ZONE 82
13. SMOOTH CRIMINAL 88
14. EMPTY ROOMS 94
15. ROCK AND ROLL DREAMS COME THROUGH 102
16. DON'T STOP ME NOW 112
17. NEW KID IN TOWN 120
18. TRAGEDY 126
19. GIVE ME THE NIGHT 134
20. RADIO GA GA 142
21. MONEY, MONEY, MONEY 153
22. BRASS IN POCKET 162
23. GO WEST 170
24. RIVER DEEP—MOUNTAIN HIGH 177
25. NEW YEAR'S DAY 184

26. PUMP UP THE VOLUME	190
27. DON'T YOU WANT ME	196
28. ONE DAY I'LL FLY AWAY	205
29. FAME	213
30. THE SHOW MUST GO ON	220
31. LEAVING ON A JET PLANE	226
EPILOGUE: WHERE ARE THEY NOW?	230
PLEASE REVIEW THE POMEGRANATE BUSKER	231
SOUTH PACIFIC SHENANIGANS	232
PHOTOS TO ACCOMPANY THE POMEGRANATE BUSKER	233
MUSIC TO ACCOMPANY THE POMEGRANATE BUSKER	234
DISCLAIMER	235
BOOK 1 IN THE SERIES: THE COCONUT WIRELESS	236
BOOK 2 IN THE SERIES: THE SCENICLAND RADIO	238
ALSO BY SIMON: AN ENGLISHMAN IN NEW YORK	240
ABOUT THE AUTHOR	242
ACKNOWLEDGEMENTS	244
WE LOVE MEMOIRS	245

The Pomegranate Busker

A Travel Adventure in Search of New Zealand Rock Stardom

1. THE ONE AND ONLY

Today, I will be successful.
　There's nothing more I can do to prepare.
　I've polished my act.
　I've learnt all the right music.
　I've rehearsed all the correct lyrics.
　People ask me to play at their birthday parties, their New Year's Eve celebrations, their street carnivals.
　Me.
　Simon Michael Prior.

My brand's heard on media broadcasts.
　My name's displayed in newspapers.
　Radio stations interview me about my background, my favourite songs, my opinion of New Zealand life.

Today, I will achieve my goal.
　Today, I will claim my prize.
　Today, I will earn my place at the biggest festival on New Zealand's West Coast.

I bound up the stairs to the organiser's office.
　I step through his doorway.
　And face the one man I never want to see again in my life.

2. TAKE A CHANCE ON ME

Eight months earlier.

Frank's strong, farmer's hand reached across the kitchen table to grab another of Linda's sweet, square cakes. He bit off a small chunk and turned to me.
"D'you reckon you might become a dad this year, Simon?"
 Fiona's cheeks turned an interesting shade of Kit-Kat wrapper. I glanced at my girlfriend to see if my daily *Garfield* research had distracted me from a Very Important Conversation.
 "Become a dad?" I asked.
 "Yep." Frank grinned and wiggled his eyebrows twice. "It's the term we use when you help one of our cows give birth."
 I rolled my eyes while Fiona flicked back her dark-red hair and glared at her father.
 He wiped his mouth and rubbed his hands together. "Farming in winter and spring's different from what you've learnt so far. You'll be starting all over again."
 I cupped my chin and stared out of the farmhouse window. While in our early twenties, Fiona's British visa had expired, and we'd fled our London life of skyscraper offices, restaurant dinners and underground trains, and backpacked via the Pacific islands of Tonga to arrive at her family's remote dairy farm on New Zealand's South Island's West Coast.
 The West Coast.
 An untamed, rugged 600-kilometre ribbon of land sandwiched between the soaring, snow-capped Southern Alps and the terrifying, crashing Tasman Sea.
 A place where trains and cars shared one-lane bridges, suspicious midnight milk tankers stormed down gravel driveways and nocturnal, horror-movie possums pilfered loaves of bread.

A region where car drivers exchanged secret index-finger salutes, locals regarded strangers with suspicion, and where the rural population maintained a low opinion of 'townies', but tolerated tourists, or 'loopies', so long as they spent money.

For the first months of 1997, I'd applied my London city-boy hands to the noble profession of dairy farming. Under the tutelage of Fiona's parents and her older brother, Phillip, I'd learnt to milk the Friesian herd and master the gentle art of tractor and four-wheel bike driving, always accompanied by my best friend, Jazz, the farm dog. Residents in the nearby town of Hokitika recognised me, even accepted me.

While I played at being a farmer, Fiona worked in a hardware store at a job that barely funded our grocery bill. If her parents hadn't lent us a tiny workers' hut to live in, we'd have been broke. As the shorter autumn days heralded the end of the farm's busy season, I hoped I could make time to earn extra money.

Fiona's mother cleared teacups and slid the last lemon slice onto my plate. "How's the guitar practice going, Simon? Are you ready to wow the locals with your London music?"

My lips pinched, and I shrugged. "I don't know, Linda. D'you think I'm good enough?"

Phillip laughed, and his teeth gleamed below his brown moustache. "You're certainly loud enough. I reckon you'll frighten the cows into premature labour."

I crossed my arms over my chest. "It's hard to play electric guitar quietly."

"You should approach some local publicans," said Fiona. "Ask them if they'll pay you to perform in the evenings. A talented band always attracts a crowd."

I rubbed the back of my neck and wrinkled my nose. "D'you think they'd pay me? I'm not exactly famous."

Frank finished his cake. "I've an idea. D'you want to ride along with me tomorrow? After my meeting at the abattoir, we could visit pubs in Greymouth, and I'll introduce you to the landlords. Greymouth's bigger than Hokitika, so there are more venues to choose from. I'll put in a good word for you too."

I swallowed hard. "Erm, I could do with more practice first."

"You've been practising every day for weeks," said Linda. "I reckon you're ready."

I flashed a smile at her, picked the edges off my cake and inspected the tablecloth.

I'd never played guitar in front of strangers.

But I treasured a dream.

A dream I'd sustained since I'd been glued to the BBC for the 1985 sixteen-hour *Live Aid* phenomenon.

A dream of playing guitar at a huge, outdoor event.

A dream of standing on a giant stage, gazing across a stadium of people with their hands raised in the air, waving in time to my music.

My name on billboards.

Posters.

Flyers.

I bit my bottom lip and felt my skin tingle.

Could this finally come true?

≈ ≈ ≈

The bottle of Müller-Thurgau chardonnay gloop-gloop-glooped into glasses. I replaced the screw-top while Fiona tonged spaghetti and divided Dolmio pasta sauce.

"What are you going to call yourself?" she asked.

"I'm not sure. A band's name needs to represent their music genre. People should be able to understand what they're coming to see. I mean, a disco band can't be called 'The Death Gorillas'. And a punk band shouldn't be named, I don't know, 'Cotton Candy Floss'."

She leant on a dining chair and whirlpooled wine around her glass. "You play '60s to '90s covers, right? How about a combination of the bands' names you perform? What about Buddy Mercury and the Beach Monkees? Or Elton Hendrix and the Dire Eagles? Elvis Jagger and the..." She grinned and held up her index finger. "Elvis Jagger and the Sex Beatles? I can imagine that up in lights above the West Coast pubs." She dissolved into hysterics.

I set down my glass and folded my arms. "It's a bloody good job your sister's away at college. I don't need two of you making fun of me."

Fiona laughed and wrapped her arm around my shoulders. "Sorry, I couldn't resist it. So, what will you name your band?"

"I'm not a band; I'm alone on stage, performing other people's songs. My name has to stand out. How can I differentiate myself from other singers?"

"Um, you're from London? There won't be any other English musicians here."

"Just because I'm from London doesn't mean I'm any good. I'm worried people will think they're attending a concert by some mega-famous English band such as Oasis or The Verve."

"But you should capitalise on being British. Why don't you call yourself Simon from London?"

"That sounds stupid."

"Simon the Londoner? Simon the Englander? Simon the Brit?"

"No, no, no." I shook my head and rolled my eyes. "Those are all rubbish."

Fiona rubbed her chin. She twirled red hair around her finger like a telephone cord and nodded. "I've got it. How about London Musician Simon Michael Prior?"

I frowned and tilted my head. "It's rather long-winded."

"Once you're well known, people will call you Simon Michael Prior. But if you include the word 'London', you'll intrigue them."

I flipped over a Bank of New Zealand statement and scrawled on the back:

London Musician Simon Michael Prior
Playing all your favourite hits
From the '60s to the '90s

I propped my homemade poster against the wine bottle.

I visualised it on a gigantic Hollywood billboard, outlined in thousands of flashing, neon lights.

I shook my head and twisted spaghetti around my fork.

Why would anyone pay to watch me?

≈ ≈ ≈

The landlord of Greymouth's Recreation Hotel grinned at Frank from under his grey, upturned-pudding-bowl haircut. "Mr Wall, how wonderful you're here. Are you fully recovered from your head injury? I haven't seen you for a long time."

He selected a bottle of Glenmorangie, spooned ice into two tumblers and splashed the whisky.

"Not that long, Charlie," said Frank. "I'm sure we compared notes at the Hokitika horse races in January. You gave me that tip on Moonlight Glen."

They chinked glasses. Charlie leant across the bar, and his tummy absorbed a glass ashtray. "So, d'you have any good tips for me today?"

"I'll give you a great tip. This young chap's Simon, over from London."

Charlie stuck a hand out. "Simon, is it? Pleased to meet you. Would you like a whisky too?"

I wiggled one palm at him. "Not for me, thank you."

"Simon plays guitar," continued Frank, "and he sings as well. He wondered whether you'd employ him to perform music and entertain your customers."

Charlie straightened his arms, locked his elbows and leant on his hands. He furrowed his brow and studied me. "What type of music d'you play?"

I gazed around at the sparse pub clientele on a Tuesday afternoon and tried to gauge which genre might be appropriate.

An older man wearing a flat cap occupied a chair and read the *Greymouth Evening Star*. He sipped a half-full glass of beer.

A young lady in a white blouse and black skirt polished cutlery. She glanced at me and smiled from under her dark bob.

A long-haired chap dressed in a checked shirt and work boots battled a beeping fruit machine.

Game Over. Oasis and Nirvana definitely won't be popular here.

"I perform a variety of music. From the '60s to the '90s. Elvis, The Beatles, The Rolling Stones; popular classics."

"D'you play any country and western?"

I clacked through my mental jukebox and failed to select a suitable record. "Erm, not really. It's not a genre I'm familiar with."

"Not to worry. Now, money. We usually pay musicians $350, and they perform for four hours, from eight until closing time at midnight."

Four hours? I've only learnt enough material for two. I'll have to play everything twice.

"That'll be no problem, Charlie."

Frank sipped his whisky and placed his hand on Charlie's shoulder. "You'd better book Simon quickly. He's received a lot of enquiries from other pubs, and I reckon you should be the first."

I turned and raised my eyebrows.

Jeez, Frank, hold up with the promotion. I haven't had a single enquiry from anyone.

Charlie unpinned a glossy calendar from the wall with the words 'South Island Pub and Bar Brewery Supplies' heading a photograph of beer taps. He flipped it to April. "All right, how about I book you for three weeks' time? The third Saturday in the month, and the same for the next three months. Then we'll review how you're going. If the customers enjoy you, we can keep the arrangement until the end of the year."

I swallowed hard.

Four gigs.

Three weeks until the first one.

Three weeks to finish rehearsals.

Three weeks to double my repertoire.

How will I ever be ready?

I looked Charlie in the eye and shook his hand. "The third Saturday will be fine, thanks. I can't wait to play here."

"I'm looking forward to it too. I'll place a big advertisement in the *Greymouth Evening Star* and promote you on Scenicland FM. I'm expecting a large audience for your first performance."

He picked up his pen and hovered it over April the nineteenth. "What d'you call your band?"

"Erm, London Musician Simon Michael Prior."

"I like it," he said. "The London angle should pull the crowds."

He stabbed the tack back through the calendar, and it swung against his pinboard. "Now, Mr Wall, let's discuss more important business. Who d'you favour for the Canterbury Draught autumn cup? French Treasure's looking sharp, don't you think?"

Their conversation about jockeys, horses and gambling odds zoned into the background.

I gazed at the black material hanging across the rear of the small, low stage like the Addams Family's dining-room curtains. My heart thumped, and the tops of my cheeks tingled.

In three weeks, I'd perform my first engagement as a solo musician.

Here.

At one of Greymouth's biggest pubs.

I'd stand on stage. That stage, right there.

In front of a crowd.

A demanding crowd.

A crowd who probably preferred to hear Kenny Rogers or Tammy Wynette.

A scene from *The Blues Brothers* entered my mind. The part where the band performs 'Rawhide' behind a metal cage while the audience hurls beer bottles.

≈ ≈ ≈

Charlie retrieved the empty glasses and uncorked the Glenmorangie.

"No, thanks," said Frank. "We should be going."

"Righto, Mr Wall."

Charlie turned to me. "Simon, or should I say, London Musician Simon Michael Prior, we'll see you in three weekends."

I took a deep breath and puffed my cheeks out. "You won't regret it, Charlie. I'm sure we'll have a great night."

Frank pushed the pub door.

"Charlie's an old friend," he said, turning the Honda's ignition key. "He'll look after you."

"Thanks for the introduction. I hope I'm ready in three weeks' time."

I plugged in my seatbelt, tipped my head back and closed my eyes while Frank drove away from the kerb and cruised slowly down Greymouth's main street.

Rows of wooden houses sheltered in the shadow of the mighty mountains, their peaks concealed by thick, grey cloud. Frank's windscreen wipers failed to compete with the West Coast rain as cars and trucks slooshed spray onto the pavements. I counted on my fingers and added up my songs over and over in my head.

Now what do I do? I haven't rehearsed enough material for a four-hour concert.

Frank swung the wheel to the left and parked abruptly. "Before we drive home, we'll pop in here."

He stepped out of the car and nipped around the bonnet to open my door.

I wrinkled my forehead at a swinging pub sign.

Frank grinned. "Ready for some more promotion?"

The bright interior of the single-storey Australasian pub contrasted with the Recreation Hotel's dinginess. Groups of customers leant against tall tables, and gamblers shoved coins into annoyingly joyful slot machines as if the Mint were going out of business and money would soon be in short supply.

"G'day, Frank," said the barman. "What'll you have?"

"A single malt, please, Dermot." He turned to me. "Same for you, Simon?"

"I'm fine, thanks."

Dermot popped a bottle open and splashed golden liquid into a glass. "What brings you to Greymouth today, Frank?" He pushed back his unruly, black hair and wiped his hands on a towel. I noticed an anchor tattooed on his short, muscular forearm.

"Dermot, this young lad's Simon; he's a musician from London staying with me. He thought you might book him to play guitar at your pub."

"From London, hey? That might draw the crowds. What sort of music d'you play?"

I clasped my hands and leant forward on the bar. "I perform popular classic hits. Chuck Berry, The Kinks, Oasis, Nirvana. Everything from the '60s to the '90s."

"D'you play any country and western?"

I need a better answer to this question.

"Um, no, I don't, Dermot. It's not terribly popular in London."

"You'll need to learn some if you hope to have any success on the West Coast. All right, we'll give you a go. I normally book a band once a fortnight. We've already engaged The Boogie Brothers for this Saturday, so how about three weekends' time?"

"Sorry, Dermot. I'm already booked that night."

This is going well. I'm so popular, I'm turning business away.

"Are you? Where are you playing?"

"The Recreation Hotel, just up the road."

"Shit, really? I'd better put you on before Charlie does. We'll book you for the Saturday before. Two weekends' time."

"Erm, sure. Sounds good."

"How much is he paying you?"

"Simon asks $350 for a four-hour performance," said Frank. "Pretty reasonable, considering you're getting a musician from London. He's come a long way to play for your customers."

Dermot spun a red pencil on the ends of his fingers, and it slipped off and vanished under the till. "I don't care where he comes from, Frank, so long as he earns his money."

He turned to me. "All right. We'll see you in two Saturdays. I'll put some ads in the *Greymouth Evening Star*. What's your band's name?"

"Umm, it seems to be London Musician Simon Michael Prior."

"Blimey. That's a bit formal. I'll advertise you as The Pommy Busker. And see if you can learn some bloody country and western."

Frank tipped his glass back and plonked it on the bar.

"Thanks, Dermot. Simon'll attract the patrons; he puts on an enjoyable show."

He turned around and led me outside.

I opened the car door and slumped into the passenger seat.

I now had twelve days.

Twelve days until my first performance.

Twelve days to polish my music.

Twelve days to learn more songs.

I pressed my palms to my eyes and leant back.

Twelve days.
And what on earth does pommy mean?

≈ ≈ ≈

Cold.

Dark.

Damp.

The shorter, mid-autumn days meant the sun hadn't risen over the mountains by the time the cows arrived for morning milking. Light spilt from the hut door as I stepped out and huffed warm air into my cupped hands.

"Here, Jazz, here, Jazz."

The dog's paws scuffed the gravel. He leapt on the back of the four-wheel bike, and I felt his warm breath on my ear. The bike's lights didn't work, so I peered into the predawn at the fence posts and crept along the farm track. The electric fence click-click-clicked as it short-circuited against the wet grass, and I inhaled the ever-present scent of farm. At this time of year, the cows waited calmly and quietly at the paddock entrance, so I unclipped the gate, and their shadowy forms exited the field. The heat of two hundred black-and-white mammals thawed the air.

I followed the stragglers into the shed as Phillip attached the milking machine to his first 24 customers. The radio accompanied the milking machine's hum.

"Thanks for those news updates, Patricia. You're listening to 93.1 Scenicland FM. It's ten past six, and once the sun peeps over the Alps, we're headed for a high of nineteen degrees. Right now, it's a chilly five Centigrade so wrap up warm while we play Blondie's 'Heart of Glass'."

"Morning, Simon," said Phillip. He marched up and down the concrete channel between the two rows of cows and removed the milking machine from their udders, as I prepared to squirt the ochre-coloured, anti-mastitis disinfectant.

"Wow, removing the cups already?" I asked. "They've finished quickly."

"At this time of year, they don't produce much; we'll milk them once a day from tomorrow. The cows are all in calf, so give it a few weeks, and we'll stop milking completely."

I frowned and pinched my bottom lip. "How does New World supermarket keep the fridges full in winter if the cows don't give any milk?"

Phillip laughed. "Milk for the shops comes from town-supply farmers. They have two herds on rotation, so they can produce all year round. We only need one for our butter and baby powder business."

I waited until Phillip rinsed cow-muck from his hands with a little hose.

I needed to ask him a vital, non-farming question.

3. THE KING OF
WISHFUL THINKING

"Phillip, d'you ever go out in town to see music?"

"I used to, before I was married."

"How does it work? Do people drink at one specific place where there's a band playing they want to hear?"

"No, they mill about a bit, drift from pub to pub. If they're enjoying the entertainment, they'll stay longer. A rubbish band will empty a pub pretty quickly."

I shut the gate after the first set of cows had departed and jumped back into the trench. "What music do people enjoy?"

"I don't know these days. When I used to visit pubs, the bands mainly played golden oldies: '60s, '70s, rock n' roll. West Coasters don't enjoy anything too recent."

Oh great. Bang goes my Nirvana and Oasis repertoire. I'll need to learn more Cliff Richard.

He gave a slight smile. "Country and western's popular. Especially Kenny Rogers. You'll do well if you play anything he sings."

I shook my head and crossed my arms. "Phillip, I'm happy to play '60s and '70s music, but I have my principles."

Phillip laughed. "I'm sure you'll be fine."

I sprayed the udders and opened the gates to let the next 24 cows trot to their paddock.

Country and western. Pppfff. I'm never playing country and western.

≈ ≈ ≈

Hokitika's single hardware shop contained everything anyone might require that didn't fall into the categories of food and drink.

In the unlikely event a customer simultaneously needed a canteen of dinner cutlery, a chainsaw, a kiwi-shaped cushion, a fax machine and a filing cabinet, the staff of Renton's Hardware would fulfil their requirements.

I stood at the counter while the shop assistant served another customer. A scent of leather and oil permeated the air, and a typewriter clacked from a back room. The customer departed, carrying a new drill in one hand and a new welder in the other. The assistant smiled at me.

"Are you here to see Fiona? She's in the office somewhere. Just a tic; I'll fetch her."

He pushed down on the shop counter and hobbled through a rear door.

I flicked through a brochure featuring fascinating photos of heated towel rails and soap holders. The assistant returned.

"She won't be long." He stacked advertising pamphlets and rearranged a display of Dulux sample paint pots multiple times, as if he were rehearsing a complicated chess strategy.

Fiona marched in and narrowed her eyes at him. "Was that Mr Marriot you served?"

"Yes, his daughter's having a baby. D'you remember her? Lisa? She's called Lisa Turnbull now, of course."

Fiona shook her head minutely. "Um, I don't think I do. Did he charge those power tools to his account?"

"He did. Is everything okay?"

"He hasn't settled up for two months. I'll call and ask him to reduce his balance. Please don't let him have anything else." She glanced at a clock behind the counter, then at me.

"Hi, Simon. D'you want to grab some lunch later? I take a break at twelve."

"Okay, I'll stroll around the town. See you soon." I pushed the door to the street, pulled my collar up and sprinted between the dripping shop awnings.

The principal thoroughfare of Revell Street ran parallel to the beach. Staff at the Southland Hotel lifted chairs from table tops and set out menus as they prepared for lunchtime service, while Scenicland FM blared from speakers mounted in an alfresco area's ceiling at an unjustifiably loud wattage for a space devoid of customers.

A poster in the window depicted a man dressed in a Stetson, a black waistcoat, tight black jeans and pointed cowboy boots. He leant against a telephone box and wore an electric guitar angled towards the pavement. Bold writing announced: Popular Christchurch guitarist Chris Whitehorse—appearing here this Saturday.

I glanced at the open door and bit my nails.

I have to ask if they'll book me. I can't rely on Frank's horse-racing friends for all my business.

My heart whumped in my chest as I crossed the threshold, and I almost turned around and walked out again as if I'd entered accidentally. A waitress in a black apron dealt beer mats like a croupier serving high rollers in Monte Carlo.

"We're not open yet, sorry," she yelled above the sound of Kim Wilde's 'Kids in America'.

Deep breath.

"I'm looking for the manager."

"D'you mean Mr Dalton?" She pointed. "Try reception. Go back outside, around to the front of the building and through the glass doors. He'll probably be there."

≈ ≈ ≈

The young receptionist smiled professionally at an elderly couple waiting at her desk. "Good morning, sir, madam. How may I help you?"

A gold badge on her white blouse advertised her name as Cherie, and she displayed several pens hedgehogged into her blonde bun. The male half of the couple detached his flat, tweed cap and placed it on the reception desk, concealing a small, chrome-coloured service bell.

"Our room," he announced.

It'd been over a year since I'd heard a slow, rural, Yorkshire accent, and the sound transported me to a world of sheepdog trials, Wensleydale cheese and *Last of the Summer Wine*.

"Yes, our room," echoed his wife. She successfully augmented the word 'yes' with a bonus syllable.

"There's a problem," said the Yorkshireman.

"Yes, a problem," repeated the lady. Her tufts of white hair had been cut by someone not best qualified for the task in a style that could accurately be described as West Highland Terrier.

"Oh?" said Cherie. She drew her eyebrows together. "What kind of problem?"

"It's the bed."

"Yes, the bed."

I realised their conversation would consume a significant chunk of my life, but I couldn't wait to hear more.

"Can you not do 'owt about the bed?" the man asked.

Cherie tilted her head to one side. "What's wrong with your bed exactly?"

The male guest turned to his partner. He lifted his chin. "I would have thought it's obvious what's wrong with t' bed, wouldn't you, Edna?"

"Yes, Reg, obvious," said Edna.

The conversation paused like a religious intercession, and I wasn't sure who'd dare to speak next.

"Well?" asked Cherie. "What's wrong with the bed?"

Reg shook his head as if he were dealing with an extremely dim child. "The window, of course."

"Yes, the window," said Edna.

Cherie held out her hands face up. "Is there a problem with the window as well, sir?"

Reg turned to Edna. "There's nowt wrong with the window, is there Edna?"

"Yes, nowt wrong," said Edna.

Cherie drew in a breath and held it briefly. "Sir, exactly how may I help you?"

"For goodness' sake," said Reg. He tapped his index finger on the counter three times. "The bed. It's too close to the bloody window."

Cherie stuck out her bottom lip and blew a puff upward. She extricated a ball-point pen from her bun, scribbled on a square of yellow, sticky paper and affixed it to a whiteboard, under the label 'maintenance'. "I'll send a porter to your room and see if there's anything he can do."

I realised the last thing she wanted was to utter the next sentence, but her professional courtesy prevented her from avoiding it.

"Will that be all, sir?"

I felt her mentally duck under the counter.

Edna took Reg by the elbow. "You were going to tell her about the tea."

"Ahh, yes," said Reg, ominously. "The tea."

"Have you run out of tea bags? I can give you some more." Cherie opened a cupboard and slid out a cardboard box with 'Dilmah' printed on the side.

Reg pointed a long, bony finger. "There's the trouble. In black and white."

Cherie turned the box around and inspected the writing. "It's Dilmah tea, sir. Very popular. It comes from Ceylon."

"Exactly," said Reg. "That's the problem."

"Sorry, sir," said Cherie. "I'm not sure I understand."

"The tea," said Reg. "For goodness' sake, the tea."

"Yes, the tea," said Edna.

Cherie's wide eyes and clenched teeth indicated she really wanted to violently throttle them, resign her job and run away down the street. "What about the tea?"

"It's not Yorkshire tea. Have you no Tetley? Or Taylors? I can't be drinking this foreign stuff."

The temptation to point out both Tetley and Taylors grew in India itched at me.

Cherie replaced the box in the cupboard. "Sorry, sir, we provide Dilmah. I'm sure New World supermarket sells other brands. It's across the road. You could buy some there?"

Reg replaced his flat cap and tugged it down on his forehead. "I know where the supermarket is."

Cherie strained out the next words with every ounce of patience she possessed. "Was there anything else, sir?"

"Yes," said Reg. "It's raining out."

"It is that," said Edna. "Raining out."

Cherie stood on tiptoe, stretched her neck and peered behind them through the glass doors. She smiled slowly. "I'm sorry, sir. I'm happy to help, but I can't do anything about the weather."

Reg looked at her as if she were a complete idiot. "I don't want you to do anything about the bloody weather."

She shook her head and blew through her lips like a horse. "What, sir, do you want?"

Reg shook his head slowly. "It should be obvious to you that we need an umbrella."

"Yes, an umbrella," said Edna.

Cherie sighed and reached into a bucket behind her. She tugged out a green umbrella. I desperately hoped she would tell Reg where he could stick it.

"One umbrella, sir."

"Right you are," said Reg.

He turned to Edna. "Shall we find some proper tea?"

"Yes, proper tea," said Edna.

She took her husband's arm, and they departed through the doors behind me.

Cherie shook herself like a dog waking up from a nap, and I permitted her a moment to recover before I approached the desk.

"Good morning, sir," she said. "How may I help you?"

"Hello, is Mr Dalton around? The manager."

"He's out at the moment. Is there anything I can assist with?"

"Erm, well, I wondered if you book bands to play in the bar?"

"We do, on Saturdays. Are you a band?" She seemed relieved my enquiry didn't include beds, windows or tea.

"Yes, I'm a musician from London. I'm living in Hokitika now, so I'm local."

"Oh, that's handy. We usually have bands from Christchurch. What sort of music d'you play?"

"I perform all the popular covers from the '60s to the '90s. The Beatles through to Oasis."

"That sounds perfect; the younger crowd here love to boogie. Could you give me your business card?"

I made a show of patting my pockets. "Sorry, I don't have one with me."

Note to self: print business cards.

She passed me a pad entitled 'Things to do today'. "Write your name and phone number, and I'll give them to Mr Dalton when he returns. He keeps a list of bands somewhere." She pulled a second pen from her bun collection.

I wrote: London Musician Simon Michael Prior. Based in Hokitika. '60s to '90s music. Tel: Hokitika 735.

She turned it around and read it. "Thanks, Simon. I know he's already arranged someone for this weekend, but I'm sure he'll be able to fit you in soon."

"Fantastic, thank you."

≈ ≈ ≈

Yes!

I punched the air and grinned as I ran across the road, dodging puddles. A poster on the door of the Westland Hotel advertised a band called Big Wheelie and the Hubcaps.

Excellent. This place employs musicians, too. In we go.

"Hello?" I called to the empty bar. A second room contained a vast, empty, 1970s English village hall area, with a large stage positioned at one end fronting a threadbare orange carpet.

"Hello?" A vacuum cleaner hummed a very very long way away. I decided to return later.

The Commercial Tavern stood opposite the supermarket, in a row of buildings between a bakery and a bottle shop. I peeked through the glass door and twisted the door handle. A lady wiped tables with a dirty cloth. I glanced at the windows, but I couldn't see the street through the browny-yellow nicotine residue.

"Hello, I'm looking for the manager."

"That would be me." She amassed empty glasses, some of which seemed to contain dregs from Dickensian times.

"Oh, right, erm, I'm a local musician. I wondered if you'd be interested in booking me to perform here one weekend?"

"Nope. No call for bands. Too bloody expensive, you lot. And too loud. My customers don't want to shout at each other." She carried the glasses behind the bar and turned her back to me. I concluded our conversation had ended.

A sign at the next corner announced: 'Ocean View Backpackers: Dormitory Accommodation and restaurant'.

A Backpackers' hostel. Maybe they book bands?

The most wonderful smell of freshly fried bacon and the sound of people's voices emanated from behind a small bar area with one beer pump and a fridge.

"Hello?" I said. I stuck my head across the bar and looked left and right. "Hello?"

"Won't be a minute," said a lady's voice. I inhaled cholesterol while I waited, then she materialised and wiped her hands on a tea towel.

"Good morning. Are you looking for accommodation?" Her fluffy blonde hair cascaded over her turquoise jumper and framed red cheeks with broken veins.

"Erm, no. I'm a local musician. Do you ever book bands?"

"Hang on. I'll fetch Rick." She turned around and shouted, "Rick," then exited to continue sizzling forthcoming coronaries.

I heard heavy boots clump downstairs and briefly appreciated how Jack felt at the top of the beanstalk. A pair of blue jeans appeared followed by a checked shirt containing a tall, muscular man with shaggy hair and a brown moustache. I couldn't help humming 'The Lumberjack Song' by Monty Python in my head.

"Can I help you?"

"Hello, Rick, is it? I'm Simon, a local musician, and I wondered if you ever booked bands to keep the backpackers entertained. I come from London originally, and I can play music they'd know from home."

Rick leant on his arms. "That sounds interesting, but it's the end of the season and we don't have many guests. How much d'you charge?"

"Erm, well, the pubs in Greymouth pay me $350 for the evening."

"That's a lot. Especially at this time of year. Sorry."

He turned his back to me and placed his foot on the first stair.

4. CENTERFOLD

"Rick, hang on."

He turned and raised his eyebrows.

"I'll drop the price to $250 for the off-season. If you like what I play, we could discuss regular performances in the summer."

"All right, why not? I enjoy a bit of music myself. D'you have a card?"

"I don't, but I'll give you my phone number."

He passed me a beer mat and a pen.

≈ ≈ ≈

Fiona paced outside Renton's Hardware. She glanced at her watch, flipped her umbrella open and marched across the road towards me. "Far out, Simon; where've you been? We'd better grab lunch; I have to be back at work by one."

"Sorry, sorry. But guess what I've been up to? So, after I left you.."

"I can't hear properly over the rain. Let's buy something from the bread shop. Tell me about it there."

Preston's bakery lured us in with amalgamated fragrances of bread, coffee and a subtle essence of Cadbury's chocolate. I breathed in through my nose and attempted to retain the scent as long as possible while we queued behind customers interspersing gossip with taking decades to select which loaf they desired.

Fiona peered around the line and licked her lips. "I'm hanging out for a sausage roll. What about you?"

"Sure, anything. Can I tell you about my morning now?"

"Oh, yes. What have you been doing?"

"I've visited some pubs in Hokitika to ask if they book bands."

"Wow. Did you have any success?"

"The landlady of the Commercial Tavern wasn't interested."

"I'm not surprised. I don't know anybody who goes there."

"And I didn't find anyone at the Westland, but the Southland and the Ocean View Backpackers asked for my phone number. They might book me in a few weeks. Actually, they wanted my card, but I don't have any. D'you know anywhere locally that prints business cards?"

"I could make them in the office when the boss isn't around. Let me know the text you need, and I'll type them."

"Wow, thank you."

The queue snailed forwards as slowly as if we waited for a spin-drier in a launderette. I rubbed my chin.

"D'you have a photocopier at work too?"

"Of course."

"How big can it copy?"

"A3, I think. Why?"

"I don't suppose you could run me off some posters?"

"Probably. What d'you want on them?"

"Umm, maybe a photo of me with my guitar? I saw a picture in the Southland's window of a country and western musician. He wore cowboy clothes and leant against a phone box."

Fiona furrowed her brow and pursed her lips to one side. "Why don't we photograph you on the farm with the mountains in the background? That'll differentiate you from the Christchurch singers."

"Good idea. I'll ask your mum to take some later."

We reached the counter. "Two sausage rolls, please," said Fiona.

I pointed into the glass cabinet. "And a caramel slice. In fact, make it two caramel slices."

"I don't want a whole caramel slice," said Fiona.

"I know. But I want to eat all of my one."

≈ ≈ ≈

I entered the farm kitchen after afternoon milking and paused as Frank clicked the knob on his dented, silver radio.

"..and they're under starter's orders, and we're off for race nine at Timaru today, the Autumn Mobile $5000. Class Bay's looking good, followed by Super Nugent as we head for the first turn. Magic Marker's posing a threat on the inside, then it's Willie The Kid and Viewfield Chief.."

I gazed out of the window, clasped my hands in front of me and watched rain clouds drift across the Southern Alps, obscuring all but the foothills. Phillip drove past on his motorbike, and I smiled as Jazz bounced up and sprinted after him.

"..Classic Melody's losing the lead; Pardon My Dust's having a run, chasing Class Bay. Pardon My Dust's coming up the outside, we're on the final straight and it's Class Bay neck-and-neck with Pardon My Dust, Classic Melody's got nowhere to go, Class Bay and Pardon My Dust cross the line together. Classic Melody takes third, but we'll have to study the official photograph to see who placed first. While we wait, some results in from.."

Frank switched off the radio, screwed up a small piece of paper and flung it in the general direction of the fireplace. He looked up at me and smiled. "Not the outcome we wanted in the last race, Simon. What are you up to?"

"Frank, which is your tamest cow?"

Frank removed his spectacles.

"What d'you mean by tame? They're all domesticated."

"I mean a pet. A cow you can stroke."

Linda entered and caught the tail end of our conversation. "Why d'you want to stroke a cow?"

"I don't want to stroke one. But I need to design some posters, to advertise I'm appearing at pubs, and Fiona thought it would be a good idea if I had West Coast scenery, to differentiate me from Christchurch musicians. I want to find a cow who'll stand still for a photo."

"There's Gladys?" said Frank. "One of the older cows. She'd be the calmest." He grinned. "Although she won't be accustomed to being a bovine Marilyn Monroe."

Linda laughed. "Fetch your camera and grab your guitar. Let's stroll out to the herd and find her. We'd better be quick, before the rain comes."

We stepped outside as Fiona pulled up. She tilted her head and offered a bemused smile. "Where are you all going?"

"We're going to photograph Simon with a cow," said Linda, as if this piece of farming activity occurred every Tuesday afternoon.

"Why?"

"For his music poster."

Fiona grinned and turned to me. "I suggested your picture needed West Coast scenery. I meant mountains, or driftwood or something. But I suppose a cow would be even more appropriate. I have to see this. Wait for me; I'll change out of my work clothes."

≈ ≈ ≈

The herd stood scattered around the paddock like black-and-white paint-spatters on a Jackson Pollock canvas. I waited with my guitar around my neck and glanced around self-consciously while Frank unfastened a latch and swung the metal gate.

Fiona backed away. "I'll watch from this side of the fence. I'm not going in with the cows. They're scary."

"Gladys isn't scary," said Linda.

"What does she look like?" I asked.

"She's big and black-and-white," said Frank.

I rolled my eyes. "That should make her easy to find."

"There she is," called Linda. She strode through the herd and placed her hand on an animal, which lifted its head in mild surprise, then resumed tearing at the grass.

Frank stood with Fiona and chuckled at the sight of me walking through a field of dairy cows with an electric guitar slung around my neck.

He leant on the gate and smiled. "You'd better make friends before explaining her assignment."

I approached Gladys and experimented with patting her huge, black head. She didn't seem to mind, so I wrapped my arm around her neck.

Linda waited a few metres away. "Are you ready for the photo? This is a good angle; it'll have Camelback Mountain in the background. Say 'cheese'. Three, two, one.."

I heard the shutter click.

"Will that be okay?" asked Linda.

"Umm, could we snap her looking at the camera? Can you walk around so you're photographing her front?"

Linda circled Gladys. Gladys decided she didn't want to be left out of this highly enjoyable game and rotated, so she stood consistently side-on. I held her neck and failed to restrain her. Frank turned away and covered his mouth.

"It's not funny," I said. "This is a serious matter." I glanced at the sky. "Hurry, before it rains."

"She doesn't want to be photographed from the front," said Linda.

"Fiona," I called. "Can you distract her? Make her look towards you?"

Fiona blew raspberries at Gladys. Gladys completed a further rotation and bent her head to eat more grass.

I tugged at Gladys's head, to no effect. "It's not working. I need her looking into the lens."

Frank doubled over with laughter and banged helplessly on the gate with his fist. Gladys found this unexpected activity intriguing.

"Linda, quick. She's looking."

Click.

Gladys became bored with being Friesian Miss April 1997 and ambled away. Frank put his hands on his knees and coughed.

"Are you okay, Dad?" asked Fiona.

He recovered, leant on the gate and shook his head. "I never thought in all my days as a dairy farmer I'd see such a sight."

"Could we please take a couple more photos?" I asked. "In case the ones with Gladys don't work."

Linda posed me against a dead tree.

"Stop smiling," said Fiona.

"It's force of habit, to smile for a photo."

"Try to look serious and moody. People will think you're a comedy act."

I tried to look more moody.

Fiona giggled. "I can't wait to see how these come out."

Raindrops spattered on the grass, so we abandoned Gladys and her friends and jogged back to the farmhouse.

≈ ≈ ≈

Linda set down plates of casserole at dinner. "You had a phone call earlier, Simon. A John someone. I wrote down the number."

"Thanks, Linda. I'll ring him back after dinner. This stew looks yummy; I can't let it go cold." I forked some meat and sauce and wiped my mouth with a paper towel.

"There's blueberry pie and ice cream too," said Fiona.

"Well," said Frank. He poured two whiskies and slid one towards me. "Blueberry pie. What a way to celebrate the launch of your new career."

"D'you have any bookings yet?" asked Linda.

"He does," said Frank. "I introduced Simon to Charlie at the Recreation Hotel and Dermot at the Australasian, and they've both employed him."

"I hope you can find better venues than those," said Linda. "Greymouth pubs are full of old men discussing horses and gambling."

Frank grinned at her. "Hang on, Linda. When did you last visit a pub in Greymouth?"

"A long time ago. And I've no intention of repeating the experience."

"When are you playing your first gig?" asked Fiona.

I sipped the whisky and tried not to grimace. "I'm at the Australasian on Saturday week, and the Recreation the week after."

"Fantastic," she said. "D'you feel confident?"

"Not really. I'm glad I don't have a booking this weekend. I need all the rehearsal time I can get."

"I'll heat up the pie," said Linda. "Here's the phone number for that John chap." She handed me a scrap of paper, and I stretched the phone's cable into the hall, closed the door and dialled.

"Hello," yelled a lady's voice. "The Southland Hotel. Can I help you?" She sounded like she was standing in the House of Commons during a particularly unruly debate.

"Can I speak to John?"

"Shaun?"

"John."

"Hang on, I'll take this in the office."

Click.

Silence.

Another *click*.

"Sorry, it's noisy in the bar. Who did you want?"

"John, please. He rang me earlier."

"Oh, Mr Dalton. Hold on, I'll fetch him."

Pause.

A distant noise of conversation, then a slammed door. "John Dalton speaking."

"John, hi. Simon Michael Prior, returning your call."

"Simon, I found your name on a piece of paper left with my receptionist. Have I rung the right chap? D'you play music?"

"Yes, John. I play guitar, and I sing '60s to '90s covers. Everything from The Beatles to Oasis."

"Oh, okay. That'll have to do, I suppose. Could you play at my pub in Hokitika on Saturday? I had a Christchurch musician booked, but his van's broken and he's cancelled. We're the busiest venue in town and we attract a good crowd on the weekends. I need a band to keep them entertained."

My insides quivered.

"Saturday, John? D'you mean this Saturday?"

5. IN THE AIR TONIGHT

I grasped the phone receiver with one hand and scraped through my hair with the other.

"Yep," said John. "This Saturday, at the Southland Hotel, eight until midnight. $350 and I'll shout you a feed and a beer. Is that okay?"

I clenched my teeth and sucked in a breath. "Erm, yes. Of course. Sure."

"Great," said John. "See you then."

He hung up. I sagged back against the wall and slumped to the ground.

Five days.

Five days to rehearse.

Five days to learn enough songs to fill four hours.

I pushed myself to my feet and carried the phone back into the kitchen.

"Who was that?" asked Fiona.

"Oh, a pub I talked to earlier. They wanted to know what kind of music I played."

I darted a glance around the room. Linda removed puddings from the microwave. Frank read the newspaper. Fiona flicked through television channels.

This needed to be kept quiet.

I couldn't tell Frank and Linda.

I couldn't tell Fiona.

I couldn't tell anyone that this Saturday, I'd be playing at the most popular pub in Hokitika.

What if I'm the rubbish band that empties the place?

≈ ≈ ≈

Fiona returned from work the next day to find me seated at our table, knee-deep in a snowdrift of scrumpled paper.

"What on earth are you doing? Are you writing a book?"

"No, I'm noting down all the songs I play by category. I need enough material for four hours' entertainment. And I'm trying to decide in what order to play them." Another screwed up page joined the pile on the carpet.

Fiona cracked open a bottle of Müller-Thurgau and glugged it into two glasses. She sat down beside me and rested her hand on my shoulder. I indicated the top of a new list.

"I'll kick off with something loud and lively, to grab everyone's attention. How about 'High Voltage' by AC/DC?"

"You're more likely to drive people away by starting with that. Don't forget, a lot of these pubs serve food. Why not begin with background music for those still dining and keep the louder stuff for when the younger crowd arrive."

"Oh, right. Quiet music to start." My shoulders slumped, and I discarded another sheet.

"Give me your song list," said Fiona. She ran her finger down it. "You can't play Radiohead's 'Creep' too early. There's a rude word in it. Save that for when people have sculled a few drinks."

"Erm, okay."

"'Under the Bridge' by the Red Hot Chili Peppers? That's about heroin addiction, isn't it?"

"Well, yes, but it's a great song."

She continued reading. "You'll need to leave 'Am I Ever Gonna See Your Face Again?' until much later in the evening. There's some audience participation in there which might offend."

"There is?"

"Yep. And the same with Smokie's 'Living Next Door to Alice'. People here add an additional chorus with vulgar words."

"They do?"

"Yes, don't play that until the end of the night. It could cause you trouble."

Fiona sipped her chardonnay. "You've got some great songs here. I think you should start with 'Wonderful Tonight' by Eric Clapton. Or 'Every Breath You Take' by the Police. Then ramp up the tempo gradually as the evening progresses."

She lay her head on my shoulder. "Are you going to play our song? 'Romeo and Juliet'."

I stroked her hair. "I think I'll reserve that just for us."

Fiona picked up her glass and departed to the bedroom. I tore off a new sheet of paper and wrote:

1. 'Wonderful Tonight'.
2. 'Every Breath You Take'.

I shrugged and shook my head.

How could playing 'Living Next Door to Alice' cause me trouble?

≈ ≈ ≈

Friday.

24 hours.

24 hours until my appointment at the Southland Hotel.

24 hours before my first ever performance as a solo rock star.

I stood in the bedroom and blasted out every song. Twice. In the order I planned to perform them. I squeezed my eyes closed and imagined a packed venue with hundreds of fans climbing over each other to see me; coloured spotlights flashing, people dancing and singing, tills dinging with record-breaking beer and wine sales. I opened them and wondered if I should have asked for more money. Jazz rested his head on his paws, raised his eyebrows and inspected me. The invisible crowd cried out, "More, more."

My dress rehearsal finished with Joan Osborne's 'One of Us'. I waved my arm above my head, unslung the guitar and called out to Jazz and my other forty thousand devotees, "Thank you very much, Madison Square Gardens. You've been amazing. See you next time. Goodnight." I exited stage left into the rock star's dressing room, previously known as the hut's toilet.

I stared into the mirror.

This is it.

You're a guitar hero.

You're a rock legend.

You're a superstar.

Linda opened the hut door. "Is this a suitable break in the concert? D'you want some lunch, if your throat's not too sore from singing?"

Madison Square Gardens evaporated in a whirl of ticker-tape.

"Sure, thanks. I'll come over."

I rested my guitar in its stand, switched off the amplifier and followed her to the farmhouse.

"How's rehearsal going?" asked Frank.

I employed decades of Jenga experience to remove the biggest cheese sandwich from the bottom of a stack in the centre of the table.

"Not bad. I'm still not sure I've enough material for four hours. But I'm as ready as I'm going to be for tomorrow night."

"Tomorrow night?" asked Frank. "What's happening tomorrow night? I thought your first performance wasn't until next weekend in Greymouth?"

Oops. Me and my big mouth.

"Um, I'm playing at the Southland, in Hokitika."

"You kept that quiet," said Linda.

"Err, I received a last-minute booking."

"Well," said Frank. "I'll have to come along and watch."

"I'd prefer you didn't; I'm extremely nervous."

Linda answered the phone and passed it to me. "Fiona for you."

I held the receiver. "Hello?"

"Is there something you haven't told me?"

"Um.."

"Something you've arranged for this weekend?"

"Ah.."

"Something happening at the Southland tomorrow night?"

"How d'you find out? I didn't want anyone to know."

"Turn on the radio."

"Now?"

"Yep."

"Erm, okay."

I replaced the receiver. Linda tilted her head and frowned at me. I shrugged.

"Fiona wants us to switch on the radio."

Click.

"You're listening to Scenicland FM. That was 'More Than a Woman', by the Bee Gees. We'll head over to Patricia for the lunchtime news, right after these messages from our sponsors."

I glanced at Frank and Linda. We stared at the radio expectantly, as if it was about to explode.

"Get your beef and onion sausages, only twelve dollars a kilo, when you buy two kilos or more from West Meats' butchers. Pop in this afternoon and receive an entry for our meat tray raffle with every purchase. West Meats' butchers, on the Kaniere Junction Road."

"That reminds me," said Linda. "I must buy some sausages."

"Shh," said Frank.

"Renton's Hardware, for all your building, farming and DIY requirements. New range of Stihl chainsaws just in. Renton's, your friendly, family-owned hardware store in Hamilton Street, Hokitika."

"That's a point; I need more chainsaw oil," said Frank.

"Shh," said Linda.

"Why not have a meal this weekend at the Southland Hotel? Call us today and book a table. We've entertainment on Saturday night from London Musician Simon Michael Prior, playing all your favourite hits from the '60s to the '90s. The Southland Hotel, Revell Street, Hokitika."

I clamped my hand across my mouth.

Oh, shit.

The kitchen door flew open, and Phillip kicked his boots off. "G'day, Simon, the postman gave me the *West Coast Times*. You're a celebrity." He spread the newspaper on the table, flopped it over and pointed to an advertisement on the back page.

My name in bold writing.

'World famous top London Musician Simon Michael Prior, appearing at the Southland Hotel this Saturday night. Come down and enjoy the best of the '60s to the '90s. Happy Hour from five until eight p.m.'

"World famous?" Linda laughed. "Top London musician? That's the last time I believe anything I see in the paper."

I re-read the advertisement.

Twice.

Me.

World famous.

I had no chance whatsoever of keeping my debut performance secret.

≈ ≈ ≈

I wiped my sweaty hands on my Levis, entered the Southland Hotel's rear door and approached the bar while 'Total Eclipse of the Heart' played from the ceiling speakers.
"Hi, I'm here to see John."

The barman slammed the glass-fronted fridge and lifted an empty Speight's beer crate onto the counter. "He's not here. Can I help?"

"Erm, I'm the musician booked for tonight."

The barman turned to his left, studied a poster on the wall and stuck out his bottom lip. "Chris Whitehorse? All your favourite country and western hits?" He glanced back at me. "You don't look like your picture."

"I'm Simon Michael Prior. John told me Chris couldn't come, so he's booked me instead."

"Oh. Hi, I'm Scott. So, what sort of music d'you play?"

"The classics. The '60s to the '90s; from The Beatles to Oasis. I'm sorry, I don't know any country and western."

"Thank goodness," said Scott. "I can't stand it. I've no idea why John keeps booking country singers. You'll be great. Something different. The young crowd here'll love you. Bring in your equipment and set up in the corner."

He indicated a small, slightly raised area with two tables set out for dining. An older man wearing a threadbare jacket sat at one. He contemplated a partly consumed beer and didn't seem to be entirely awake.

"Bill, move your butt," shouted Scott. "The musician needs to set up."

Bill obediently pushed down on the table, picked up his beer and relocated. I averted my gaze at his eviction, but I hoped he wasn't tonight's typical clientele.

My guitar, amplifier and speakers overflowed the small area, and I sticky-taped several hundred yards of electrical cable to the carpet. A red light glowed as I flicked the switch on my amplifier. I approached the microphone, cleared my throat and said, "one-two, one-two." I had no idea what this meant, but I'd seen it on *Top of the Pops*.

Scott gave me a thumbs up, so I threw my guitar around my neck and strummed a test chord, which sounded ridiculously loud in the empty pub. I squeezed my eyes closed and breathed in deeply.

I'm ready. Bring it on.

"D'you want anything to eat?" asked Scott.

My heart raced, and I wasn't sure I could manage anything.

"Erm, yes, please. Something small."

"How about a West Coast delicacy? A whitebait sandwich?"

"Yum. Thank you."

"Have a seat. I'll bring it over. D'you want a beer, or anything else to drink?"

"Could I just have a lemonade, please?"

A tall man approached me as I sat at a vacant table. "G'day, Simon. I'm John Dalton. Thanks for filling in at short notice." His bald, freckled head shone, and his ginger moustache covered his upper lip.

"No problem, John. Thanks for booking me." My mouth had dried up, and I licked my tongue around my lips.

"It should be a good night," he said. "Make sure you play some country and western."

"Erm, sure. I'll find something."

Scott placed the sandwich and drink in front of me. I picked up my food, stared at a mirror fixed to the pub wall and cupped my chin in my hand.

A scene over ten years ago entered my mind.

6. WHEN WILL I BE FAMOUS?

My father drives me home after school rugby practice. I crouch in the passenger seat and loosen my spiked boots. He gearsticks through second dramatically, and the handle above the window becomes suddenly vital as we centrifuge around a one-way system.

"I can't believe you'll be fourteen next month, Simon. Is there anything special you'd like for your birthday?"

I clench my teeth, suck in a breath and raise my eyebrows. "Erm, there's a guitar in the window of Johnson's Music Shop. A black one. I've had my eye on it for ages."

"A guitar? Are you sure? You already own a guitar."

He waits in pole position at the traffic lights and Schumachers the throttle.

"This one's a Fender electric guitar, Dad. It's different. And it has a Marshall amplifier with it. You can buy them as a package."

"An electric guitar and amplifier. Hmm. You'll have to wait and see."

I raise my eyes to the sky and mutter *please* under my breath.

≈ ≈ ≈

I dream of stardom.

My school careers counsellor asks my class to complete a form entitled 'What do you want to be when you grow up?'. I write 'musician'. I also add I've no intention of growing up.

I form a band at school and make the ambitious and audacious statement we'll headline at the Hammersmith Odeon on my eighteenth birthday.

We live a very long way from Hammersmith.

What we don't possess in quality, we make up for in quantity. The band flaunts three electric guitars, two unnecessarily loud Marshall amplifiers and vast second-hand speakers, which cause the family's Austin Allegro to creak alarmingly under their weight.

Our instruments and accompanying accessories connect with several miles of wires and questionable electrical arrangements.

We rehearse in the attic of my father's vicarage. The phone rings.

"Hello, this is the vicarage," he answers.

"It's sacrilegious," rants a nearby resident's voice.

"An unholy row," shouts another.

"That bloody racket's disturbing the Sabbath," yells a different neighbour, during one Sunday afternoon practice session when 'Smoke on the Water' vibrates through the walls several hundred times.

Rehearsals abruptly terminate when my father answers the door to a young policeman who requests in an embarrassed voice if we could please turn the music off.

We never perform on stage.

The band disperses long before my eighteenth birthday.

And the Hammersmith Odeon isn't even called the Hammersmith Odeon any longer.

7. BLAME IT ON THE BOOGIE

Scott removed my plate and cutlery. I watched the bar clock's minute hand and bit my nails.

7.53.

7.54.

7.55.

Dining couples scooped ice cream from bowls. A waitress dressed in a white top and black skirt balanced dishes up her arm.

7.56.

Three farming-attired men leant at one end of the bar engaged in a conversation that required multiple gesticulations and back slaps.

7.57.

Bill departed. The empty glass remained as an epitaph to his solitary afternoon.

7.58.

I slung my guitar around my neck, wiped forehead sweat with my sleeve and stepped up to the microphone. My gaze darted around the sparse population. Thankfully, no-one had noticed me.

7.59.

Scott refilled a customer's sparkling wine. He nodded at me and rotated a knob on a black box marked 'Pioneer'. The background music evaporated, and the bar conversation became more obvious.

8.00.

I felt an all-over tingle of adrenaline, cleared my throat and spoke into the microphone as quietly as possible. "Good evening, everyone."

Pause.

My knees shook, and I tongued my lips constantly as the percentage of moisture in my mouth declined below zero.

"It's great to be here at the Southland Hotel. I'm London Musician Simon Michael Prior, and I'll be entertaining you through 'til midnight."

I turned around to inspect my speakers, as the voice coming from them didn't sound like mine.

As Fiona had suggested, I started by strumming the opening chords of the ballad Eric Clapton had written for Pattie Boyd, 'Wonderful Tonight'. One of the dessert diners looked up, then continued conversing with her partner. The waitress placed plates on the serving hatch and stacked a pile of menus. The three farmers' conversation continued.

Here launcheth the career of London Musician Simon Michael Prior.

≈ ≈ ≈

9.00.

I'd played through half my songs, which presented a serious problem as three hours remained until John expected me to finish. The diners had progressed to after-dinner coffee, and the farmers had progressed to another jug of beer.

I finished my first set with Sam Cooke's '(What a) Wonderful World', ambled into the bathroom and faced the urinals. A middle-aged man stood next to me.

"You're the musician, right?"

"Yep. Is it always this quiet? This is the first time I've played here."

This is the first time I've played anywhere, but we won't mention that.

"It's only nine o'clock," he said. "People don't leave home until later. The pubs put on bands to attract people to come out earlier, but no-one ever does."

He zipped himself up, swished his hands under the taps and exited. I leant on the sink with both arms and stared in the mirror. My lips pressed together, and I breathed out through my nose.

Where were the adoring crowds, the dancing audience, the party people waving their hands in the air?

Come on, Simon. John's paying you to play music. Get back out there.

The increase in noise became apparent as soon as I opened the door.

≈ ≈ ≈

A large group of skimpily dressed young ladies surrounded a woman robed in an outfit manufactured entirely from tin foil, and a handwritten sign Sellotaped to her back displayed the word 'bride'. I strode up to the stage and slung on my guitar.

What can I play to suit a hen party?

I ran my finger down my song list, smiled, and launched into the opening riff of the crowd-pleaser 'Mustang Sally'. The hen party abandoned the bar and danced in front of me. As I reached the chorus, two of the ladies broke away from the group, stepped up next to me and sang the refrain into my microphone.

Wow, audience participation. That's more like it. This is turning into a great night.

I planted my feet wide apart and shared a grin with the bride-to-be, who danced unsteadily in a circle of sisterhood. 'Mustang Sally' segued into 'Love Is in the Air'. An appropriate song for the occasion, and I felt sure the hen party would enjoy it.

They had other ideas. The tin foil-clad bride and her entourage sculled their drinks and continued their crawl to a different pub. Love was no longer in the air, or on the dance floor. None of the remaining customers showed any interest in tripping the light fantastic.

≈ ≈ ≈

11.45.

The clientele of The Southland Hotel had increased to around twenty people. Nobody had clapped or cheered, or, except for the hen party, danced or sung along. I shook my head slowly and began my winding-down songs ready for the midnight finish.

I hope the Greymouth gigs are livelier than the so-called busiest venue in town.

Halfway through 'Moondance' the pub doors swung open, and a crowd of young people surrounded the bar. Scott suddenly needed six arms and twenty hands as he filled several glasses of beer, flipped lids from small assorted-coloured bottles of Smirnoff cruisers and juggled coins, notes and till buttons. I bit my lip.

Damn. I need something up-tempo, but I've played all those songs.

I restarted 'Mustang Sally'. An impromptu dance floor fanned out as bleached-blonde girls hung off each other, yelling the refrain while young men swigged from drinks and shuffled at the fringes. Hands waved in the air, pelvises thrust, hips wiggled. The grin on my face spread so wide I struggled to sing properly.

This is how it's supposed to be. Why couldn't everyone have arrived at eight?

Multiple choruses later, I finished the song and bowed left and right as the audience cheered and clapped.

11.55.

I'd reached the bottom of my list so I strummed the Beatles' song 'Here Comes the Sun'. The crazy antics continued in front of me. One girl swung her date around with their mouths limpeted, crashing into others and distributing drinks over an already sticky dance floor. The exuberant frolicking would have perpetuated if I'd played Beethoven's 'Moonlight Sonata'.

Midnight.

I raised my fists in the air, lifted my heels and spoke into the microphone. "Thank you very much. I'm London Musician Simon Michael Prior, and you've been a great audience. Goodnight." I turned around and rested my guitar in its stand.

"Is that it?" asked a young brunette with a hickey on her neck. She placed her hands on her hips and leant forwards.

"You're not finishing now?" said her friend, lipstick smeared around her face as if she'd had a nasty accident in the House of Fraser make-up department. "You've only played for ten minutes."

I started to explain I'd been performing since eight o'clock, but Scott turned the black knob, and 'Break My Stride' sounded from ceiling speakers, so the girls turned away from me and danced to that.

I unplugged my gear and packed it away. John Dalton approached.

"Sorry about the quiet night," I said. "It didn't liven up until the end."

He handed me folded bank notes. "I told you. You should have played more country and western."

I looked at my feet, shoved the money in my pocket, and exited stage left.

≈ ≈ ≈

CRACK

    CRACK CRACK

    CRACK

    CRACK CRACK CRACK

    CRACK

I sat bolt upright in bed and darted glances left and right. *What the hell's that?*

Fiona's side of the duvet lay folded back, and I heard water cascading. I ran into the bathroom and shouted at the shower. "Fiona, did you hear gunshots? Someone's firing guns."

She pushed back the plastic curtain and tugged a towel from a hook on the wall. "Did you say something?"

I peeked through a gap in the bathroom door. "I think I heard gunfire. Listen—there it is again."

Fiona laughed and flicked back her wet hair. "It is gunfire. It's duck shooters; the season starts today. Be careful if you're out on the farm."

"Duck shooters?"

She rubbed the towel over her head and strode into the bedroom. I darted glances out of the windows.

"Yep, the place'll be crawling with idiots carrying shotguns," she said. "Some of them can't fire straight for toffee. Make sure they don't shoot you or Jazz by mistake."

She pulled on a long-sleeved top and a Fiona-shaped lump expanded in one arm, so I laughed and guided the top over her head. She shook out her long, dark-red hair and grinned. "How'd it go last night at the Southland?"

"Okay I suppose." I tugged on a T-shirt and trousers. "Actually, not terribly well. Hardly anyone turned up until the last fifteen minutes, and then they complained I finished too early."

"We're a tough crowd, us West Coasters. I'm sure your next gig'll be busier. Where is it?"

"The Australasian, in Greymouth, on Saturday. They also want me to play country and western but I don't know any. I don't like it, either."

"I reckon you'll be fine. There are medical staff from the hospital opposite the pub who drink there. They'll be happy with your song list." She lay back on the bed and buttoned a tight pair of Levi's.

I formed a steeple with my fingers.

The final fifteen minutes of the previous night.

The crowd.

The dancing.

The atmosphere.

I pulled Fiona up from the bed and hugged her. "I can't wait to play again. Hopefully, you're right about The Australasian."

She wriggled out of my embrace, picked up a pair of gold earrings and stabbed them into her lobes. "D'you want to come to my primary school teacher's farewell? It's at the school hall this afternoon. We need to bring a plate."

"Sure. Do we have to take a knife and fork as well?"

"A plate of food. Not an empty plate. You've lived here long enough to know that."

I grinned and winked.

≈ ≈ ≈

Fiona's old school comprised a two-roomed, white, wooden building which stood by itself in slightly overgrown grounds. I grabbed Fiona's arm as we entered and spoke close to her ear.

"This is the smallest school I've ever seen. How many children attend here?"

"In my final year, the roll comprised two classes of about fifteen kids each." She scanned photos pinned to a corkboard. "I don't think there are as many now. So many young families have moved away."

We placed our donation of Linda's homemade cakes on a table laden with crockery decorated in numerous 1950s flowery designs. I scooped a handful of Bluebird potato chips.

Fiona indicated a bowl of off-white goo. "There's dip to go with those."

"This stuff? What is it?"

"Kiwi dip. Made with Maggi reduced cream and Maggi dried onion soup."

I selected the largest chip in the bowl and experimented with the dip. As the goo possessed the viscosity of elderly house paint, the chip snapped, and I glanced around to ensure no-one had noticed me rescue the broken piece. "Yum, that's different."

I shovelled more with the next chip. "I'm enjoying this dip. Err, isn't Maggi a Swiss company? Shouldn't it be called Swiss dip?"

"It's Kiwi dip. Every New Zealander knows that."

We swung around to the familiar sound of a knife tinging on a glass. Three ladies stood at the front. One cleared her throat and spoke. "Thank you all for coming today."

Her straight, grey hair fell evenly around her face as if someone had placed a plastic bucket over her head and cut along the edge.

"It's wonderful to see so many staff, parents and students at Paula's send-off, and especially former pupils." She turned to Paula. "It demonstrates the affection that the school community holds towards you."

As I fell into none of the categories she'd mentioned, I loitered at the back and helped myself to more chips and Kiwi dip while everyone's attention was diverted.

"Paula, would you like to say a few words?"

Paula's wavy brown hair dangled on either side of her heavy-rimmed glasses. "Thank you, Barbara." She paused and surveyed the audience. Her eyes watered, and it occurred to me the last time I'd seen a teacher cry was when Mr Peake marked my history exam.

The salty chips had made me thirsty, and I searched around the table for something to drink. Four bottles of Oyster Bay Sauvignon Blanc stood at the end. I presumed it wasn't my place to uncork them, so I poured water from a jug into a plastic cup.

"May I thank Barbara and Deirdre for your friendship over the last twenty years." She nodded left and right at her colleagues.

The speech progressed as expected, and I wondered how many chips I could reasonably consume without it being too obvious I'd eaten almost all of them. I picked up another one and shoved it in the dip.

Paula continued. "It's been wonderful being part of this school community for so long, and I.."

The lady seated on the other side shoved her chair back. Her nostrils flared, she bared her teeth and cut Paula off mid-speech.

"Sorry, Paula. I know you feel I shouldn't mention this, but I want everyone to be aware you're not leaving of your own free will."

8. THE POMEGRANATE BUSKER

I paused with a chip halfway to my mouth.

Ooh. Here's where the afternoon becomes interesting.

Paula wiped her eyes, sighed and faced the lady who had spoken. "Deirdre, I had hoped we weren't discussing this here."

Deirdre flicked her wavy, ash-blonde hair and shook her head. "I'm so upset you've been forced out of a job you loved. I think it's disgusting the school governors haven't supported you after all these years of service. Those responsible should hang their heads in shame." She turned to the assembled parents and pupils, many of whom began an intense study of the carpet pattern. "I felt everyone here needed to know."

She sat down, looked at her feet and folded her hands in her lap. Paula didn't seem sure how to reply and opened and closed her mouth like a pet goldfish. Barbara stood up again and blinked rapidly.

"Right. Well, it's marvellous to see so many of you from Paula's past and present. She'll look forward to catching up over some nibbles."

People clapped, turned to each other and murmured amongst themselves. I hoped some of them would help me eat the food.

Fiona looked at me, then down at the empty bowl and raised her eyebrows.

I grinned with clenched teeth and slid my eyes left and right. "Erm, would you like a glass of wine?"

"You grab one," she said. "You must be thirsty after eating all those chips. I'll find you in a minute; I want to chat with some old friends."

Deirdre poured Oyster Bay from the four bottles. "Hello," she said. "Have we met? Are you a former pupil or a parent?"

"Neither," I said. "I'm not originally from the area. I'm here with my girlfriend today; Paula used to teach her."

"Oh, goodness. I'm sorry you had to witness my brief outburst."

"But you gave the best speech," I said. "The most passionate. People will remember yours."

"I'm glad someone agrees with me. Many people will never know the full story."

Hmm. Curiouser and curiouser.

I rubbed my chin. "If you don't mind me asking, why is Paula resigning?"

"I suppose I can tell you, as you're not really connected to the school. Earlier this year, one of the families whose children attend.."

Fiona tapped me on the shoulder. "Sorry, Simon, could I introduce you to my old classmistress?"

"Yes, sure. Excuse me."

I resigned myself to never solving the Scooby Doo Mystery of the Disappearing Teacher and followed Fiona across the room.

"Hi, Mrs Jacobs," said Fiona. "D'you remember me?"

"Goodness me; Fiona Wall. It must be over ten years since you sat in my class. You can call me Paula now we're both adults. I understand you've been living in England."

"That's right, but I'm back. This is Simon, from London. I brought him home in my baggage."

"Hello, Simon. How are you enjoying the West Coast?"

"Very much, thanks, Paula. It's beautiful."

"And what have you found to occupy yourself here? Are you milking Frank's cows?"

"Yes, and I'm playing guitar in pubs. I performed at the Southland last week."

"Goodness, I feel honoured to have a famous musician at my little do."

I ran my hand through my hair. "I wouldn't consider myself famous. Not yet anyway."

"I think you're being modest," said Paula. "What type of music d'you play?"

"'60s to '90s covers, such as The Beatles, The Rolling Stones, Oasis."

"Why don't you post an ad in the *West Coast Times* stating you're available for weddings and 21st birthdays? You're bound to pick up a few bookings. Winter's coming; there'll be a lot of celebrations while the farmers enjoy time off."

"That's a good idea. I'll visit the newspaper offices."

I left Paula and Fiona to reminisce as I'd discovered an overlooked bowl of chips and dip.

≈ ≈ ≈

The newspaper office occupied a tiny, cream-coloured building in the centre of Hokitika. Paint peeled off the window frames and black dots of dead flies decorated pigeon-grey net curtains. No sign indicated which organisation inhabited the premises. I tapped three fingers flat on my lips.

Is this the right place?

A wooden door creaked at the top of three concrete steps, and I peeked around it. "Hello? Is this the *West Coast Times*?"

A small man with a bald head looked up. He wore a strange contraption across his forehead, with a monocle folded across one eye. "It is. May I help you?"

His black waistcoat and brown Corduroy trousers reminded me of a Charles Dickens character.

"Could I place a small ad please?"

He shuffled paper around his desk and unearthed a pad entitled 'classifieds', then enjoyed an equivalent challenge to excavate a pen. "Right. Small ads. Birth, death or marriage?" He winked. "Hatched, matched or dispatched, as we say in the trade."

I shook my head. "None of those. I'm a musician, and I want to announce I'm available to play at people's parties."

"Hmm. I wonder which section that would go in?"

He flipped to the back page of the previous day's edition, frowned and scanned from the top down to the bottom. "It's not items for sale, is it? How about goods and services?"

"Is there anything else to choose from?"

"Items wanted?"

I twisted my head to read the paper. "Could you put it in the entertainment section?"

He paused and pressed his lips together. "That's reserved for venues advertising events."

"But I am advertising an event. It's just the event doesn't have a date yet."

He sighed and ticked a box next to the word 'entertainment' on his pad.

"D'you have your ad copy?"

I passed him my piece of paper. He held it at arm's length.

'Are you planning a 21st or wedding? London Musician Simon Michael Prior is now based in Hokitika and will provide the best '60s to '90s music for your function. For bookings, call Hokitika 735.'

He counted the words aloud. "$35, please. It'll appear in this Friday's edition."

≈ ≈ ≈

Saturday morning.

The Australasian tonight. I hope it's busier than the Southland.

The butterflies in my stomach either promenaded with excitement, terror or a combination of both. I practised singing scales. I'd no idea what I hoped to achieve by doing this, but I'd seen a documentary about Pavarotti and figured this was the right thing to do.

Linda knocked on the door, and I paused mid-arpeggio. "Simon, Carol McCloud on the phone."

"Who?"

"Carol McCloud. She's the town's ladies' hairdresser."

"Oh, okay, I'm coming."

Why would the ladies' hairdresser call me? Has Fiona got her head stuck in the dryer or something?

I sprinted to the farmhouse.

"Hello?"

"Hi, Simon, this is Carol," she said, as if we knew each other. "I've seen your ad in the *West Coast Times*. My son's having his 21st birthday in a few weeks. Could I book you to play some music? It's at the Kowhitirangi Hall out in the valley so you won't have far to travel."

"Wow. Erm, yes, of course."

I smiled and gave a thumbs up to Linda, who furrowed her brow.

"It's on Saturday evening, the 31st of May."

I covered the mouthpiece. "Linda, could you find me a pen and paper?"

Linda passed me a pad titled 'groceries'. I wrote '31st May—McCloud party. Valley Hall.'

"That'll be fine, Carol. I'll arrive during the day and set up my equipment. Does he have any favourite songs?"

"So long as his friends can have a dance, play anything. Bring Fiona, of course. She knows the birthday boy."

"Excellent. Thanks, Carol. I'll see you then."

I replaced the receiver and grinned.

"What did Carol want?" asked Linda.

"She's booked me to play music at her son's 21st, at the end of May. It's at the hall up the road."

"The entire valley'll be there. Brandon's a talented rugby player, and everyone knows him."

"Wow. I'd better practise more songs."

Linda grinned and shook her head as I ran back to the hut.

≈ ≈ ≈

A young man wearing a checked shirt and jeans stood in front of me at the Australasian Hotel with his feet planted wide apart and his fists on his hips. "Are you the Pommy Busker?"

I took a step back. "Erm, I'm the musician tonight, yes. Simon Michael Prior, from London."

"The paper said you're the Pommy Busker. Are you any good?"

He picked up a half-drunk beer which I guessed wasn't his first. I looked at him and decided it didn't matter how I replied, he'd hate me anyway. "You'll have to stay for the evening and find out, won't you?"

He laughed and held out his hand for me to shake. "You're all right, for a pom. I'm Jason. D'you take requests? I always ask bands to play my favourite song."

"Sure, which is it?"

"'The Gambler'."

"'The Gambler'?"

"Yeh, y'know, Kenny Rogers. Everyone knows it."

Everyone except me.

I pinched my lips and shook my head. "Umm, I don't know any Kenny Rogers." I grinned. "How about Kenny Loggins?"

"Bloody hell. I've never met a musician that can't play 'The Gambler'. It sounds like you need to do your homework."

He spun on his heels, pulled out a ten-dollar note and slammed his empty glass on the bar. I shouldered my guitar and stepped up to the microphone. "Good evening, everyone, and welcome to The Australasian Hotel."

Jason put his hands to his mouth and shouted. "It's not the Australasian Hotel, you posh idiot, it's the bloody Aussie. Everyone calls it the Aussie. Gees, where'd Dermot find you?"

My cheeks tingled, and I took a deep breath. "Right. Welcome to the Aussie. I'm London Musician Simon Michael Prior; I'll be with you until midnight, so grab a beer and enjoy the sounds."

"I am grabbing a bloody beer, you git," said Jason. He grinned, nodded dramatically and gazed around the pub to ensure everyone had heard him. As the customers continued to play pool and insert money into slot machines, I gathered they expected this behaviour from him.

I sighed and kicked off with R.E.M.'s 'Losing My Religion'.

≈ ≈ ≈

Bar staff grabbed glasses, poured drinks and took money. A strip of coins along the edge of the pool table reserved queue position for the next game. The volume of the conversation, not all of which came from Jason, competed well with the sound of my speakers.

But no-one clapped.

No-one sang along.

No-one cheered.

No-one danced.

Why did I ever want to be a musician?

I finished with 'Yesterday'.

"Thank you very much. You've been a great audience. I'll see you next time."

Jason approached me. "You can't finish now. You haven't played 'The Gambler'. I told you; it's my favourite song."

I shrugged and turned my palms upwards. "And I told you I can't play 'The Gambler' and I don't even know it."

Jason jabbed his finger at me. "How can you not know it?" He called over his shoulder. "Dermot, can you book a proper band next time?"

Dermot stepped out from behind the bar and grasped Jason's arm. He steered him around tables and chairs to the exit door. "You've had enough, Jase. Time to go home."

He shut the door and addressed me. "Come and see me when you've packed up, and I'll give you your money."

I smiled and nodded. "Thanks, Dermot. It's been a good night, hasn't it?"

He gave me an odd look and returned to the bar.

≈ ≈ ≈

Linda pressed toasted cheese and tomato sandwiches while Fiona brewed tea.

"How did you go at the Australasian?" asked Frank. "Did Dermot pay you okay?"

"Oh, he paid me, but I'm not sure he was happy. I think I need to swallow my pride about country music before I play the Recreation Hotel next weekend. Some bloke kept asking me for a song called 'The Gambler', and I'd never heard of it."

"Everyone knows 'The Gambler'," said Fiona. She assumed a Dolly Parton accent and sang the first few lines.

"I've got it on a record," said Linda. "We can listen later."

"And that same bloke kept calling me a pom, or pommy. It didn't sound complimentary."

"It's short for pomegranate," said Frank. "Aussies and Kiwis called the early English immigrants *poms*, because in the heat their skin turned the colour of pomegranates. And 'pomegranate' almost rhymes with 'immigrant'.

"Right. Well, he wasn't exactly friendly."

Fiona plopped down next to me at the kitchen table. "Can I read your song list again?"

I de-origamied a piece of paper from my back pocket and spread it in front of her.

She ran her eyes down it. "But you already play country and western. 'Take Me Home, Country Roads'? That's as country as anything."

"Really?" I tilted my head and raised one eyebrow. "I thought country music was all about your dog dying and your wife running off with your next-door-neighbour."

"'Take It Easy'? Eagles fall into the country category. And look, 'Achy Breaky Heart'; people will line-dance non-stop when you play that."

I leant in to study the list. "So, if I played all of those, and I learnt this song 'The Gambler', I could tell publicans I have a country and western repertoire?"

"Of course. Problem solved."

Linda answered a knock at the kitchen door to an unshaven man dressed in a khaki shirt and trousers, who offered her a plastic carrier bag. "Frank said we could shoot on his land today, so here's a duck to say thank you."

He handed her the bag. She hesitated, opened it slowly, and investigated the conglomeration of feathers and blood as if he'd presented her with a human skull.

"Erm, thanks," she said. "We'll enjoy it."

She shut the door and narrowed her eyes. "I really don't want to pluck and clean this. I'll put it in the bin."

"Simon and I love duck," said Fiona. "We used to eat it in London's Chinatown, accompanied by pancakes and yummy sauce."

Linda passed the bag to Fiona. "You can cook it then."

≈ ≈ ≈

Multiple diners occupied tables in the Recreation Hotel, and groups of men and women leant on the bar.

Two overhead televisions transmitted a sports game, and cheers or groans echoed around the room, depending on which side gained an advantage. I stood on the low stage with my hands on my hips.

This is going to be a great night. I can feel it.

The waitress ferried empty plates past me. "Hi, are you Simon? I'm Floss."

Her short, black, Jennifer Aniston bob curled under her chin.

"My brother, Dave, works in the kitchens. Once we finish our shift, we'll join you for a boogie. I can't wait."

I smiled and gave her a thumbs up. "Nice to meet you, Floss. At least there'll be two people in the audience."

"I reckon you'll have a lot more than two; the pub's busy tonight. I must carry on."

She bumped through a swing door. I glanced around at the clientele as I positioned my amplifier and plugged in my guitar. A group of six older ladies wore a uniform of cowboy hats, waistcoats and knee-high boots. I wondered if they all worked at a rodeo. Two middle-aged couples sat at a table. I reckoned they might be American from their appearance and demeanour. Several smaller groups of younger people drank, chatted and watched the sport.

I didn't observe any Jason-equivalents.

The rodeo ladies watched me tape down my cables. One of them nudged her neighbour and pointed.

Charlie lined up glasses and filled them from beer taps. "G'day, Simon." He glanced up at the television. "It'll be full time in ten minutes, and then I'll mute it."

"No problem. Give me the nod."

The suspected Americans turned around in their chairs as I passed.

"Where are you folks from?" I asked.

"We're from a city called Bellingham," said the larger man. "You might have heard of it."

He removed his grey, large-lensed spectacles and sucked on one of their arms.

"Sorry, I haven't." I said.

"The northernmost city in the lower 48," said a lady opposite him.

"North of Seattle, close to the border with Canada, in Washington State," said the other man.

"That's Washington State, not Washington D.C.," said the first man, using an explanation I reckoned he'd had to pull out his entire adult life.

"Right. Bellingham. Washington State."

"What kind of music d'you perform?" asked the lady. "Would you play some Elvis for me?"

Her thick make-up and Madonna-red lipstick reflected the wall lights next to their table.

"I can't promise to be as good as The King, but I have 'Hound Dog' in my repertoire. Shall I announce it's for you?"

The lady grinned and blinked at me several times. "Sure, honey. Say it's for Margaret. Margaret from Bellingham."

I tried and failed to impersonate Elvis Presley. "All right, Ma'am, that'd be mah pleasure."

Charlie approached. "Ready to start? I'll turn the telly off."

I walked back to my microphone and slung on my guitar.

Rodeo girls: check.

American tourists: check.

Country and western: check.

"Good evening. Welcome to the Recreation Hotel. I'm London Musician Simon Michael Prior, and this is 'Achy Breaky Heart'."

As soon as I strummed the riff, the six cowgirls stood up, marched to the front of the room and executed a perfect line dance. I watched them boot-scoot, electric slide and hip-swing and hoped I'd still be as flexible in my seventies. I planted my feet wide, pushed my chest out and belted the chorus. The whole pub clapped and fixated on the rodeo ladies as if I'd organised them as my backing dancers. I mirrored some of their less-complicated moves, and we finished the routine together.

This is fantastic. Everyone's glued to the act.

"Next, a special treat for my good friend Margaret, from Bellingham, Washington, U S of A. That's Washington State, folks, not Washington D.C."

I launched into 'Hound Dog'. The line dancers continued while Margaret's partner slapped his thigh hopelessly out of time. I completed the song and swung my arm in a circle like I'd seen Elvis do on television.

"Thank you very much indeed. Ah said, thank you very much indeed."

The American man laughed and smacked the table. He approached me and placed a five dollar bill on my guitar case.

Wow! He tipped me.

"And now, folks, 'Take Me Home, Country Roads'."

The rodeo ladies shimmied a different routine, the Americans clapped and slapped, people danced and drank. Charlie grinned, nodded and pushed two thumbs up.

This is how it's supposed to be. None of these unpopular Southland or Australasian gigs.

I finished my first set, held hands with the line dancing ladies and we all bowed as if we stood before the final curtain in a pantomime.

"I'll take a quick break, folks, and I'll be back for some more fun. I'm London Musician Simon Michael Prior; see you soon."

I switched off the microphone, placed my guitar in its stand and entered the bathroom. After a significant pee, I stood in front of the mirror and turned up my collar.

This is what I was born to do. I can't wait for the next set.

I rearranged my hair, marched out through the toilet door and stared at an empty pub.

9. THINGS CAN ONLY GET BETTER

The rodeo ladies, the Americans and the other diners had all departed. A few drinkers slouched at the bar and one couple lingered over a bottle of wine. I frowned and gazed through the entire pub at the swinging exit door.

Was I that long in the bathroom?

Floss wiped tables. She conversed with a young man who grinned through his scraggly beard.

"Hi again. This is Dave, my brother."

"Hi Dave, pleased to meet you. Err, where did everybody go?"

"This always happens," said Dave. "As soon as we stop serving food, most people leave."

He frizzed up his shoulder-length brown hair with both hands and glanced around the pub. "Don't worry, there's nothing wrong with your guitar playing. I'm sure more drinkers will come in later."

I sucked in a breath and hoped they would.

'The Wanderer' followed 'The House of the Rising Sun'. Then 'The Joker'. Then 'Free Fallin'.

I reckon I'm freefalling. Maybe I should play some New Zealand songs?

I started Crowded House's 'Weather with You'. The wine-drinking couple stood up and danced in front of me, then clapped and returned to their sauvignon blanc. I didn't want to perform upbeat songs to a three-quarters empty pub, but my selection of background music had expired a long time ago. 'I Got You' and 'I See Red' by Split Enz. More New Zealand music. 'Born to Be Wild'. 'The Boys of Summer' by Don Henley.

Four people propped up the bar.

Two people lingered over empty plates.

One old man dozed in the corner.

'Should I Stay or Should I Go?' seems more appropriate.

Floss swapped her waitress outfit for a T-shirt and jeans. She perched on a stool at a tall table with her brother. "Come on, Simon," she shouted. "Dave and I are here for a big night."

I played '(Sittin' On) The Dock of the Bay'. I arrived at the part where Otis Redding whistles, and I attempted to emulate him. My whistling sounded more like blowing raspberries, and Floss and Dave collapsed into hysterics. I discovered I couldn't whistle and laugh simultaneously, so the three of us harmonised through 'Another Brick in the Wall', 'I Saw Her Standing There', and 'Honky Tonk Women'.

Charlie waved and pointed at his wrist.

Midnight. I finished with 'Knockin' on Heaven's Door'.

"Goodnight, Greymouth. You've been a great crowd."

Floss clapped unilaterally. She stacked a beer-glass Leaning Tower of Pisa while Dave bumped the door into the kitchen.

"Not bad, Simon, not bad," said Charlie. He licked his thumb, counted out fifty-dollar notes and closed the till. "D'you want a beer?"

"Sure, why not?"

I stood next to a tall, thin man, wiped sweat off my brow and drank the beer in one gulp.

"Another one?" Charlie laughed. "Bit hot tonight?"

He poured a second one. I restrained myself from sculling it too rapidly. The thin man leant on one arm and turned to me.

"I enjoyed your music tonight, thanks."

His closely cropped hairstyle and inverted horseshoe-shaped moustache made me wonder if he rode a Harley Davidson.

"You're different from other bands Charlie books. I haven't heard some of those songs for ages."

"Thanks, I'm glad you enjoyed it." I gulped my beer.

"'Another Brick in the Wall', 'Knockin' on Heaven's Door', 'The Wanderer', those all take me back."

"Yep, they're pretty popular."

"Whereabouts are you from?"

"I live in Hokitika now, but London's my hometown."

"Gosh, that brings back memories. I lived in London in the 1970s. Carnaby Street, Piccadilly Circus, all the pubs and shops. I still have a keyring I bought at Camden Market."

He reached in his pocket and tugged out a bunch of keys attached to an enamel image of Big Ben. I pretended to show interest and hoped this chap would let me pack up without reminiscing for too long. He indicated my empty glass.

"D'you want another one? I'll buy you a drink."

"I'd better not. That was my second, and I'm driving."

"Oh, don't worry," he said. "Nobody will breathalyse you tonight."

I scratched my jaw. "How can you be so sure?"

"I'm one hundred per cent sure they won't. Among my other responsibilities, I'm the town's traffic cop."

≈ ≈ ≈

A tractor crunching gears outside the hut woke me.

Clock.

11.45.

Fiona's side of the bed lay empty.

Woah. These late nights mean I'm absent from morning milking.

I tugged on clothes, strolled over to the farmhouse and found Frank dressed in a jacket and tie and Linda threading one arm into a coat sleeve. Fiona stood back from the oven, as a cumulonimbus billowed to the ceiling. I tilted my head back and inhaled through my nostrils.

"Something smells good. What's for Sunday lunch?"

Linda buttoned her coat and checked her lipstick in a mirror. "Frank and I are eating in Greymouth with the chairman of the meat works. Personally, I'd rather stay here and have a ham sandwich, but I'd better put in an appearance. You're having duck. Fiona's plucked that bird the hunter gave us."

Fiona extracted a tray from the oven and prodded the contents with a skewer. "Come back in ten minutes. It'll be ready then."

"Sounds yummy. I'll make myself presentable."

The shower steamed, as I shampooed away the smells of stale beer, cigarettes and sweat. I closed my eyes, tipped my head back and let the water Niagara down my body.

I'd played the Southland Hotel. The crowd enjoyed my music once they'd arrived, but most of the evening I'd entertained a deserted bar.

I'd played the Australasian, where I hadn't been well received. One customer looked like he wanted to thump me.

I'd played the Recreation Hotel, where I'd started well with my newly mastered country and western repertoire, but the evening petered out as soon as it'd begun.

The big test would be next week, at Brandon McCloud's 21st birthday party. White soap bubbles vortexed around the plughole. I stood motionless until the last one evaporated.

21st birthday party. Important, special occasion. I hope I'm good enough.

I turned off the shower, sandpapered my skin with a freshly laundered towel and pulled on clothes.

≈ ≈ ≈

Fiona set down two plates of sliced meat and vegetables, swimming in a thick, orange gravy.

I smiled and wafted the rising steam with my right hand.

"Duck with orange sauce," she said. "It's the first time I've cooked wild duck."

I cut a piece and bit a corner off. "Yum. This is delicious. The sauce brings out the flavour."

I lowered my fork, frowned and gazed out of the window.

"What's wrong?" she asked.

I smiled and shrugged slightly. "I'm not sure I'm cut out to be a musician. The three pubs I've played so far haven't exactly had customers queueing down the street to hear me."

"This is the West Coast. Have you seen people queue for anything?"

"No, I suppose not. I can't wait to play at Brandon McCloud's party. I mean, everyone'll be there for a joyous celebration. They'll be in the mood for some singing and dancing."

I sliced another piece of duck. "This is yummy. You've outdone yourself. I wonder if the shooters will give us any more?"

≈ ≈ ≈

Fiona sat on the farmhouse couch the following day with a hot water bottle pressed to her stomach.

"How come you're not at work?" I asked her.

"I'm suffering from a funny tummy. It must've been something I ate."

"Oh, okay. D'you want any lunch?"

"No, thanks. There's still some of the duck and sauce left. You finish it, seeing as you enjoyed it so much."

"Oh, yes," said Linda. "How was the duck?"

"Delicious," I said. "Next time we're given one, Fiona'll have to cook it for you."

I opened the fridge, extracted a Tupperware container and inserted it into the microwave. Frank distributed the contents of a tin of Deep Cove Sardines over two slices of toast and spread the *Christchurch Press* across the table. I sat opposite him with my reheated duck.

He glanced up. "I'm attending an important conference call with the board of the meat works at three o'clock." He folded the paper and removed his glasses. "It'd be good if we could keep the background noise down for half an hour."

"No problem, Frank," I said. "I'm going to read your book about Stanley Graham."

"*Manhunt*, d'you mean?" asked Linda. "That all happened up the road here, opposite the hall where you're playing at Brandon McCloud's party. You remember it, Frank, don't you?"

"I would've been around seven years old," said Frank, "but I recall it clearly. That murder of seven police and guardsmen relegated World War II to the back pages."

I shook my head slowly. "Wow. I can't wait to read the story."

"I'll sit with you and finish my magazine," said Fiona.

Linda curled up on the couch and gathered up knitting. I read the first chapter while winter sun warmed my face. Linda's needles tapped quietly. I snuggled a cushion, leant against Fiona's lap and dozed off.

≈ ≈ ≈

Cold perspiration beaded on my forehead. I woke, frowned and wiped it with my hand. A Fred Flintstone-sized boulder had formed in my stomach.

Frank's voice sounded in the kitchen. "Frank Wall joining the call, Mr Chairman."

Sweat poured down my face.

"Brian sends his apologies today, Mr Chairman," continued Frank.

I tugged Fiona's *New Zealand Women's Weekly* away from her face.

She stared.

I stared.

"Fiona, help me."

10. IT'S MY PARTY

Fiona dropped her *Woman's Weekly*.

"What the hell's wrong? You're white as paper."

Frank's conference call continued in the kitchen. "The beef figures for the financial period weren't as high as the previous year, but we have suffered a drought, and this contributed to the lower revenue, which is expected to recover in 1997-98."

My mouth fell open, and my breathing became shallower. "Help me, Fiona. Fetch me a bloody bucket, quick. I'm going to throw up."

Fiona sprinted to the washhouse and returned with a big, metal pail. She clanged it down beside the couch.

"Now," said Frank. "If we could come to the next point, the demands from the union. As you know, Mr Chairman.."

"Huuuuuaaaaaaaggghhhhhh."

Frank's board meeting paused mid-vomit. I stared at the carpet and took short, rapid breaths.

"Heeeeuuuuggghhhh. Huuh Huuh Huueeeuuuugghhh."

Fiona ran to the bathroom, soaked a cold flannel and patted it on my face.

"Hueeeeuuuuuuuuuuuuuuuuuuugghhhhhhhh."

"My apologies, Mr Chairman, there's someone here who, err, isn't feeling well."

I sat up, wiped sweat, leant on Fiona and panted. She tugged tissues from a box.

"What brought that on?"

"I don't know. Perhaps it's food poisoning? I feel better now I've been sick."

Frank assessed whether my stomach would permit him to continue. "As I mentioned, Mr Chairman, the demands from the union for a seven per cent pay rise. We need to ensure that whatever response we give, the message is simple; no pay rise without a commensurate increase in producti.."

"Hhhoooooorrrrraaaaaagghhh."

Fiona mopped me with the flannel.

"Heuuuggghhh. Huurrugghhh."

Frank covered the mouthpiece with his hand. The conference call continued, interspersed with regurgitation. Frank replaced the receiver.

"I'm sorry, Frank," I said, as I wiped my mouth with the flannel.

"I have to say that was one of the more interesting end of financial year board meetings I've attended. What d'you think's wrong with you?"

"I've no idea. My stomach's in absolute agony. I can't bring anything else up."

I sipped water.

Linda furrowed her brow. "Did you cook that duck properly, Fiona?"

Fiona folded her arms. "Yes, I followed the guide in your English cookery book. Although the recipe gave the temperature in Fahrenheit, so I guessed at 150° Centigrade."

Linda clenched her teeth and sucked in a breath. "150° Centigrade isn't very hot. It would've needed cooking for longer."

"Oh," said Fiona. "I thought it looked pink in the middle, but I wondered if duck meat always looked pink."

I moaned, panted, and forced my head back into the tin bucket.

≈ ≈ ≈

Scenicland FM competed with the hum of the milking machine as I watched the last cows' rear ends depart the shed.

"That's it," said Phillip. "We're done." He clasped his hands above his head and grinned.

"Until tomorrow?" I said.

"Nope. Until September. No more milking 'til spring." He clicked off the machine and the radio truncated mid-scattered shower.

"What do we do over winter?" I asked.

Phillip climbed on his motorbike. "Feed the animals. And maintenance. And have a bloody rest. We've earnt it. Once the cows start giving birth in September, we'll be all hands on deck and you won't know whether you're Arthur or Martha. Could you wash the yard? Give it a good splash, then go over it with the pressure washer; we won't be cleaning it again for weeks. I'll lock in the herd."

He kick-started his bike, and cow muck sluiced down the drain as I sprayed the big hose.

≈ ≈ ≈

I crept into the farmhouse and surprised Linda in her dressing gown.

"Sorry, Linda. I thought you'd be up by now."

"We rise later in the winter. D'you want a cup of tea? I'm brewing one."

"Sure. Thanks."

Linda set down two mugs on the kitchen table. "What are today's plans?"

"It's Brandon McCloud's 21st tonight. I want to set up my gear this morning before the party people start decorating. D'you know how I unlock the hall?"

"Easy. The key's hanging by the next door house's porch."

"All right, I'll nip up there. Back soon."

I slurped the Vesuvius-hot tea as quickly as possible, ran to the hut and loaded my car.

The milk tanker entered the farm, and the driver grinned and gave me the West Coast index finger salute as we passed. I guessed he anticipated his winter break as much as the rest of the farming community. Morning mist blanketed the paddocks as I accelerated through the valley towards the ever-present Southern Alps. I hummed, tapped the steering wheel and smiled.

Tonight's going to be massive. I can't wait.

A large bush obstructed the path up to the village hall, and creepers ran across the steps and strangled the side of the building. I gazed at the field opposite, and a herd of cows gazed back. No memorial indicated the site where the deranged farmer Stanley Graham had shot seven police and guardsmen dead in 1941. His house of horrors had been razed as if it never existed.

I discovered the gigantic, metal hall key, lifted it down and weighed it in my hand as if I were a Beefeater, entrusted with unlocking the Tower of London so Her Majesty could perform a quick inspection of her crown. The key slid into the white-painted, wooden double door and clunked as it turned. I pushed, but nothing shifted. No matter which way I rotated the key, the door remained sealed. I forced the key back in the first direction, leant my shoulder against the door and shoved.

A space confronted me which no-one appeared to have visited in centuries. Shafts of light diagonalled through side windows and illuminated clouds of dust disturbed by my entrance. I sneezed and shook my head from side to side, as my footsteps clump-clump-clumped on the wooden floor. A switch by the stage at the far end illuminated dangling lights, and I smiled slowly.

Thank goodness the power's on.

Two off-white electrical sockets protruded under the light switch, and I calculated where I'd mount my speakers.

"Hi. Are you Simon? I'm Carol." A plump lady with short, dark, wavy hair materialised in the doorway. "Gosh, it's a good job I brought the Hoover." She flapped a hand in front of her face and coughed theatrically. "I reckon this place was last used at Don and Edith's fiftieth wedding anniversary."

We stepped outside into the sunlight.

"How long ago was that?" I asked.

She opened her car tailgate, tied an apron around her waist and arranged carrier bags and boxes. "Umm, Don died last year, so it must have been 1995. It's no wonder the hall's so dusty."

A pickup truck stopped behind her with two wobbling towers of chairs and trestle tables stacked precipitously in the tray.

"Oh, good," she said. "Here's Tony and George with the furniture."

We processed into the hall. I carried a speaker, the men hauled two tables between them, and Carol lugged shopping bags. Two other ladies followed and struggled with a square, white cardboard box.

"Morning, Carol," said one. "Where d'you want the cake?"

"In the kitchen, please. Be careful with it; I've had it made especially for Brandon by that lady in Greymouth. Her creations are amazing, but she charges a fortune."

I plugged in my gear while Carol and her colleagues swept and vacuumed behind me.

"What time are the guests arriving?" I asked.

"They're invited for seven. But knowing Brandon's friends, they won't turn up until at least nine. Could you start with some background music as people mingle? Then, may we use your microphone for the speeches and the cake? After we finish, you can pump out some dance tunes."

"No problem, Carol. I'll nip home and change my clothes."

≈ ≈ ≈

7.00.

Silvery-grey moonlight illuminated fields like a scene from one of the creepier Stephen King novels, and sporadic lights shone from remote farmhouses as Fiona and I sped along the country road towards the hall. We parked at the end of a line of cars and stumped towards the light spilling from the entrance.

Tables laid with platters of food edged the wooden floor, coloured streamers looped along the walls, balloons with '21' in white writing dangled from the rafters, and at the front of the stage a table displayed the gigantic, white cake, centred with red-and-blue rugby ball-shaped icing. I skirted along the buffet and smiled as I recognised my old friend the Kiwi chip and dip.

Carol tapped my shoulder. "Help yourself to a beer, Simon. Oh, hi, Fiona. Would you like a wine?"

I locked my fingers together and flexed my hands so my knuckles cracked. "I'd better not drink anything until later in case I play the wrong notes."

The amplifier click signalled the start of my performance, and I strummed quiet background music. A lady approached me between songs.

"Can you play any Cliff Richard? He's my favourite."

"How about 'Living Doll'?"

She smiled, and her eyes brightened. "Yes, please. The oldies are the best, aren't they? The music today's so repetitive. These modern groups sing the same words over and over again."

I decided not to point out that the lyrics to 'Living Doll' comprised an identical verse and chorus repeated three times and started from the beginning.

"Here's the birthday boy," said Carol, as I completed Cliff's third stanza, and she introduced me to a young man with cropped brown hair.

"Pleased to meet you, Brandon," I said. "Oh, and happy birthday."

He shook my hand and grinned. "Thanks for handling the entertainment. I'd better circulate with the older crowd. My rugby mates'll be here soon, and things might become messy."

Carol smiled and rolled her eyes.

By nine o'clock, people of all ages packed the hall, drinking, eating and chatting. I increased volume to compete with the conversation, shared smiles with guests and acknowledged smatterings of applause.

Carol stepped up to the side of the stage and yelled at me. "We'll do the speeches and cake now. D'you want to take a break and grab some food?"

I terminated 'Bad Moon Rising', pushed through the throng and selected a paper plate.

Fiona grinned at me. Her left hand gripped a champagne flute of fizzy wine so hard I worried she'd snap the stem. "You're, you're a good musish, musishian, Simon. I love you."

I stuck my bottom lip out and opened my eyes wide. "How many of those have you had?"

She wrapped her spare arm around my neck. "Don't know. Don't care. They're easy to drink." She released her grip on me and leant heavily on the table. I relocated a bowl of dip from under her arm in case she had an accident with it.

"You won't be driving home, then?" I asked.

"Nope."

She poured dregs into her glass and tipped it back. "You. You doing that."

Carol stood on stage with Brandon and a group of young men. One hijacked the microphone and enthusiastically listed several embarrassing episodes in the birthday boy's life. Brandon stood behind the cake and grinned. Carol cupped her hands around her mouth and shouted, "where's Simon?"

I stuck my arm up and waved.

"Can you come to the stage?" she yelled.

I donated my plate of sausage rolls to Fiona's alcohol-soak-up cause and squeezed through the guests to the front.

Carol bent her head to my ear. "Could you please play 'Happy Birthday to You'?"

I clenched my teeth and smacked my forehead.

Oh, no. I'm such an idiot. I didn't learn it.

"Err, no problem, Carol."

She struck a match and lit 21 candles circling the rugby ball motif on the huge, beautiful, square cake. I turned down the volume and rehearsed 'Happy Birthday to You' quietly. It didn't sound quite right, but Carol raised her arms and led the guests in a choir of birthday song, so I strummed randomly. Any chords would have worked. One hundred drunken voices drowned my playing nicely.

"Hip hip,"

"Hooray."

"Hip hip,"

"Hooray."

"Hip hip,"

"Hooray."

Pause.

"Come on, ya donk," said Brandon's friend. "Blow out the bloody candles."

Brandon leant forwards and puffed hard. One or two candles refused to go out, and he bent his head close to the surface of his immaculate, expensive, hand-crafted rugby-themed birthday cake to extinguish them.

Two of his friends met eyes, smiled and nodded. They placed their arms around Brandon, and as the last candle expired, they shoved his face into the cake. He surfaced, covered in icing like a scene from *Mrs. Doubtfire*. Carol hid her mouth with her hand, shook her head and walked away.

The lads laughed, high-fived, and fell against each other. Brandon grinned and wiped his face with multiple napkins. I struck up 'La Bamba', a dance floor formed, and the partying escalated.

≈ ≈ ≈

The older generation had departed. Brandon and his rugby friends laughed and polished off remaining beers. I searched for Fiona, but someone had already driven her home.

"You can leave your music equipment here," said Carol. "Fetch it tomorrow when we return and clean up. It's a good job the police never venture this far up the valley. Some of these chaps won't be able to see past their steering wheels." She indicated a group of lads who hung onto each other in a line and sang 'Show Me the Way to Go Home'.

"I had one beer in the end," I said, "so I'll be fine. Everyone seemed to enjoy themselves, didn't they?"

"You played exactly what I wanted. I'll tell my friends to book you for their kids' celebrations."

I hooked my thumbs into my belt loops and grinned. She opened the clasp on her handbag. "Here. For you."

I stuffed the banknotes in my pocket and bowed slightly.

"Thank you, Carol. I'm so glad you enjoyed it."

I jumped in my car, turned the stereo all the way up, accelerated home and sang along with 'We Are the Champions' at the top of my voice.

≈ ≈ ≈

Fiona opened one eye.

"What time is it?"

The alarm clock glowed accusingly.

"Ten o'clock. D'you want breakfast?"

She puffed out her cheeks like an overfed hamster. "Groooo. No, I want to die. My head feels twice as big as it should."

"I'll leave you to sleep it off."

I grabbed a coffee and some toast, hopped in the car and drove back to the hall to retrieve my gear.

As I turned a corner, something in front of me looked very wrong.

11. I STILL HAVEN'T FOUND WHAT I'M LOOKING FOR

Tangled ends of barbed wire splayed across the verge as if there'd been a jail break from Wormwood Scrubs, and an elderly Toyota station wagon rested on its side in a field. I slowed down and stared, but there didn't appear to be anyone in the car, or any people around at all. Across the road a Honda saloon lay in a ditch, with a tractor resting on top of it. I stopped, opened my car door and ran towards the accident. Dark-red stains spattered the road, but my investigation revealed no injured humans.

What happened here?

Outside the hall, ladies ferried bags and boxes, and two men hefted folded trestle tables.

"Hi, Simon." Carol waved as she unlatched her car boot.

"Hello, Carol. How are you today?"

She laughed. "I'm fine, but I don't think Brandon'll surface for a while."

I pointed over my shoulder with my thumb. "Have you seen the accident up the road, with the cars, and the tractor? D'you know anything about it?"

Carol raised her eyebrows and shook her head with her mouth in a straight line. "Typical. Jamie, one of Brandon's rugby mates, had too much to drink last night, drove home, missed a bend, smashed through a fence and ended up on his side in Ernie Smith's heifer paddock. He's unhurt, thank goodness. Just scratches."

"Yes, I saw the car in the field. But what about the other vehicles in the ditch? Are all the passengers okay? I thought I saw blood on the road."

"Jamie spooked the heifers when he crashed into their field in the middle of the night, as you might expect, and they escaped onto the road. Another of Brandon's friends came around the corner, saw the heifers in his headlights, swerved, clipped one of them and ended up in the ditch.

All the lads climbed out of the car; no broken bones. They knocked on old Ernie's door, bearing in mind this was one o'clock in the morning, and Ernie's eighty-six, and asked if they could borrow his Massey Ferguson to pull the car out. He opened his shed, one of the lads backed the tractor and reversed it into the ditch on top of the car. I don't think anyone's going to forget that night in a hurry."

I sucked in a breath and covered my mouth.

≈ ≈ ≈

Frank removed his glasses and folded the *Christchurch Press*. "I saw Tony McCloud in town yesterday. Carol's husband. He was impressed that you managed to persuade all the young lads and lasses to dance at Brandon's party. He said the chaps on the West Coast are normally reluctant when it comes to having a boogie."

"I agree," said Linda. "None of the young people want to dance. Not like us when we were kids."

She grabbed Fiona and twirled her around the kitchen, an activity that curtailed abruptly when they banged into the rubbish bin and knocked it over.

Frank furrowed his brow and tapped his flat hand on his closed mouth. "D'you remember the Wild Foods Festival? Where you ate the huhu grub?"

"How could I forget?" I said. "I recall the horrid peanut butter taste whenever I think about it."

"I reckon you should perform at next year's festival. Loads of bands appear there, but they have to be imported from Christchurch or further afield. They'd be stoked to have local talent."

My nose wrinkled. "D'you reckon I'd be able to, Frank? I've always dreamed of performing at a massive outdoor concert. But the festival bands would be so professional, so well-rehearsed. And the organisers probably require groups, not solo musicians."

"Of course you could do it. No-one will care if you're on your own, so long as you play popular songs people can dance to. From what I've heard you're pretty good at that."

I rested my arms on my elbows, formed a steeple with my fingers and stared out of the window.

I'm Brian May, on stage at Live Aid. I watch Freddie run up and down in front of the audience, brandishing his half-microphone stand. The opening drum beats of 'We Will Rock You' sound, as I gaze out at the Wembley crowd, strike a power chord, and a unison of 70,000 people cheer, clap and wave their cigarette lighters in the air.

"Far out," said Fiona. "You've played four gigs. There's a long way to go before you'll be ready for the Wild Foods Festival."

Brian May evaporated in a puff of hairspray.

"Keep at it," said Frank. "Promote your name out there; make sure everybody knows you're the best talent in town." He turned to Linda. "Who books bands for Wild Foods? Is it Mike Keenan?"

Linda called from the kitchen. "He's the event manager. But I reckon that Dennis Stark chap from the council has a say in the matter too."

"All right," I said. "I'll enquire once I've performed a few more events."

"Where's this weekend's gig?" asked Fiona.

"The Ocean View, in Hokitika. Have you ever been there? It's away from the centre of town and I'm not sure many will turn up."

"It's backpacker accommodation," said Frank, "but there won't be many tourists in winter. The chap who owns it's a gold miner. Some of his mining colleagues might drink there."

The kitchen door flew open, and Frank's newspaper flapped onto his toast. He peeled it off and scraped marmalade back onto the plate.

"Morning," said Phillip.

"Shut the door," said Linda. "It's freezing."

Phillip stepped in and closed the door behind him. "Could you feed the cows today, Simon? I want to prepare for a jet boating contest."

"Jet boating?"

I had a vision of a 1960s cartoon canoe with a space rocket attached to its stern.

"Yep," said Phillip. "I own a little boat, which I race occasionally. Today's competition's in the Hokitika river at the end of our farm track. After you've finished feeding out, you could watch the machinery dig out the course."

"Wow, I'd love to."

Plus, every rock star needs their own speed boat. It's part of the lifestyle.

"If you could hitch the loader tractor to the silage wagon, tow it up the track and feed the main herd? Then, swap over to the four-wheel bike, chuck a bale of hay on the trailer and spread it around the bulls' paddock. They're next to the river, where the race is happening."

"The bulls?"

"Yep, there are about fifty in the paddock."

I swallowed hard. "You want me to enter a field with fifty bulls?"

Phillip laughed. "They're more interested in the feed than you. Don't stand between them and the hay. Oh, and keep Jazz out of the way. They always attack the dog."

I blinked. "Um, okay. I'll fetch my coat."

≈ ≈ ≈

The tractor's engine cranked several times before puffs rose from the vertical exhaust. Jazz ran around the front wheels and barked enthusiastically as I reversed, hopped down from the driver's seat and attached the silage wagon. He inspected my hitching, and it seemed to meet his approval. I grabbed him by the scruff of his neck, and he scrabbled up beside me. Cold air chilled the insides of my cheeks as we puttered along. A fresh dump of snow had decorated the mountains overnight, and the white frosting down to their foothills contrasted against the blue sky. I grinned and felt Christmas-excitement, an anticipation which would be completely unfulfilled in this country of upside down seasons.

The cows greeted the tractor and kicked up their heels along the fence line beside the track.

"Won't be long, ladies," I called. "Special treat today. Silage for a change."

The animals stopped as they reached the gate and all mooed continually like a particularly undisciplined choral society.

My icy hands struggled to undo the catch. "All right, ladies, calm down. I'm working as fast as I can."

I pulled my sleeves over my hands and tugged desperately to curtail the din of bovine conversation. The gate swung open, and the cows shoved around the cart and licked silage from the sides. I picked up speed across the paddock and pulled the lever to release their food. This distracted the herd, as they competed for the first chunks to tip from the wagon. A big omega of steaming wet grass formed behind me, surrounded by cows feasting like lines of ants who've discovered a spilt packet of granulated sugar.

I swapped the tractor for the four-wheel bike and grabbed a bale of hay from the back of the shed. Twine cut into my hands as I heaved it onto the trailer. Jazz jumped on the bike's tray behind me and huffed chemistry experiment-sized clouds of breath. Strands of straw blew behind us as we bumped along the gravel track, and Jazz sneezed.

Fifty virile young bulls waited at the entrance to the field. They jostled and butted in their excitement to be first at the hay. I scraped my hand through my hair and sucked in.

Check your escape route, Simon.

The gate swung open, and I turned around and vaulted back on the bike in one movement. The bulls galloped behind me across the field while I performed complicated mental trigonometry to estimate their angle of attack. When I judged I'd put enough distance between me and my adversaries, I nipped to the back of the trailer. Sweat beaded on my forehead as I dismembered the hay bale and distributed it.

The twine wouldn't unpick from the second part of the bale. I tugged and tugged, then bent over the trailer, and sawed with the serrated edge of a key I'd found in my pocket. Strands twanged loose one by one.

Almost through. Quick, Simon, quick.

I glanced up. The bulls paraded towards me in a V-shape, with a large one at the point, as if they'd brainstormed a battle formation in advance.

Twenty metres between me and the leading bull.

Half the hay to spread.
Plenty of time.

12. DANGER ZONE

WHAM

A whack like a rhinoceros riding on roller skates rammed me in the backside, tipped me over the side of the trailer and jolted Jazz off the bike. Half a ton of solid bull-muscle mounted the trailer and tugged at the remaining hay while I crabbed backwards, inverted onto my knees and pushed myself up as fast as I could.

"Jazz, jump on quick."

The dog leapt on the bike, and we accelerated away from the feeding frenzy.

≈ ≈ ≈

I rubbed my lower back and stepped off the bike at the end of the track, where a digger worked the dry gravel river bed and created a wiggly channel. Besides several men with pocketed hands observing the process, a cluster of Frank's black Hereford cows leant across a fence and inspected the action. I wondered how many jet boat competitions they'd spectated, and whether one of them commentated or provided expert opinion.

Jazz sprinted off after the white powder-puff of a rabbit's tail.

Phillip tapped my shoulder. "Have you ever seen anything like this?"

"Never. How does it work?"

He pointed at a newly formed mound of pebbles. "Once the digger's finished, we launch the jet-boats into the river. We enter the course, the timer starts, and we zip around as quickly as we can. If we're the fastest to the exit, we've won."

"We?"

He grinned. "Yep. D'you want to be my co-pilot?"

Wow. A real rock star experience.

"Sure. What does it involve?"

"When I'm driving, I'm concentrating on what's happening right now. Your job as the navigator is to tell me what's going to happen next. Left bend, right bend and so on."

"How do I show that?"

Phillip demonstrated with his hand. "When the next bend is to the left, point left. When it's right, point right. I'll be driving at fifty kilometres per hour, so I'll steer wherever you tell me. If you accidentally say right instead of left, we'll end up on the gravel."

I took a step back. "Won't that wreck the boat?"

"It'll scratch it, but it's made of aluminium. We'll push it back in again. I try to avoid that."

"Um, okay. But what about the engine? The propeller?"

"There aren't any propellers. I'll show you."

Phillip led me to the rear of his pickup truck, which towed a trailer supporting a minute, stripped-down, bright-green boat. The front contained two bare plastic seats, which reminded me of the uncomfortable chairs I had to withstand during maths lessons. The right-hand one faced a steering wheel, and a tall, metal roll cage framed them. A large, impressive-looking engine poked out behind.

Phillip indicated the stern of the vessel. "The engine pushes a jet of water through this vent." He touched a black pipe which resembled a toilet's u-bend. "When I turn the wheel, the pipe points left and right. Watch." He reached over the side of the boat, swivelled the wheel, and the u-bend moved. "This means we can change direction rapidly and sprint through shallow water. New Zealand invented these boats, and they're sold all over the world."

I tapped the side twice, and the metal echoed as if I'd clanged an empty oil drum. "How fast does she go?"

"Her top speed's 75 kilometres per hour, but we won't reach anything like that today in the tight bends."

75 kilometres per hour? Definitely a rock star's speed boat.

The digger driver switched off the excavator, and the silence permitted birds to recommence conversation. He stepped down from the cab and lit a cigarette.

"Could you give me a hand?" said Phillip.

I helped him tug the boat off the trailer, and he started the engine, which sounded like a marine ride-on lawn mower.

"Jump in. We'll have a practice round." He passed me a helmet.

I held it and hesitated. "Why do I need to wear this?"

"You'll see. So, show with your hand whether I go left or right. Ready?"

I felt my muscles tense. "Erm, okay." I lifted the helmet over my head and fastened the chin strap.

We pushed the boat away from the river bank and jumped in. Phillip started the engine, water sprayed behind us and we chugged slowly towards the course entrance. The line of black cows examined our voyage as we glided upstream. I glanced at Phillip and grinned.

This is the life. I'm a rock star in my speed boat.

The jet boat entered the course, and immediately the G-force pressed on my bull bruise. We shot through the narrow channels like a scene from *Live and Let Die*. I wedged my hand behind me and held my back.

"AAAAAAAAAAHHHHHHH."

Hang on, I'm supposed to be the navigator. Shit. Is the next corner left or right?

I indicated right. Phillip turned right. My head ricocheted to the left.

I indicated left. Phillip turned left. My head ricocheted to the right.

I indicated left again. Phillip turned left again.

Sweat ran down my forehead, and I felt a familiar sensation in my stomach.

I indicated right, left, then held my hand up flat.

"Please stop," I shouted.

Phillip throttled back, and we drifted to a halt.

He looked at me and grinned. "What's wrong?"

I guess I'm not cut out for this aspect of the rock star lifestyle.

"I can't do this anymore, Phillip, sorry. I don't want to throw up in your boat."

≈ ≈ ≈

1950s London pea-soup fog gripped Hokitika that evening as I cruised along the deserted streets, watching thick smog settle between the houses. Lights peeked through the gloom from behind tightly closed curtains. The not-unpleasant smell of wood smoke permeated the car, reminding me of English garden bonfires, and I reflected on the irony of heating wooden houses by burning wood. I hoped the volunteer fire brigade wouldn't be required tonight.

A sign on the door of the Ocean View Backpackers advertised 'Free apple crumble with purchase of any main meal', which had the potential to be a bigger draw card than my music.

Rick bent over a hearth in the front bar and stoked a fire. He stood, and his checked shirt stretched around his biceps. "Evening, Simon. Set yourself up here. Guests in the dining room next door will be able to listen without it being too loud for them. D'you want me to ask Charlene to cook you some food?"

"I'll bring my gear in first if that's okay."

"Sure. Don't stress if it's not busy tonight. We don't have many customers in winter."

"No worries, Rick. I'll play a bit of background music and see how we go."

My set opened with 'Stand by Me', a nice, easy number which would add atmosphere while guests spooned their free apple crumbles. Rick poured two beers and carried them through to the diners, as Ben E. King ended, and Del Shannon's 'Runaway' began.

CRASH

A skinny, black-haired, red-shirted man flung the door open between the dining room and the front bar. He noticed me, grinned alternate teeth and gaps, joined me on stage and sang drunkenly into my microphone.

"RUNAWAY, RUNAWAAAAAAAYYYYY."

Rick, where are you? Help!

The man tugged at my guitar strap. I pulled it away, and he returned to his first love of the mic stand. He blurted the second verse of the song, which in his arrangement repeated identical lyrics to the first but with more slurring. I glanced left and right and hoped the clientele didn't mistake his tuneless singing for my voice.

No-one else in the pub paid attention, so I permitted him to continue and hoped he'd become bored with his guest artist appearance. We completed 'Runaway', and he tumbled off the stage onto the floor, picked himself up and lurched back into the dining room. As I strummed 'Wish You Were Here' shouts came from behind the door.

Charlene marched in from the back room, knocked over a stack of menus and picked up a phone. Her red face and flapping arms indicated she wasn't calling a friend to arrange a shopping trip.

What on earth happened?

Pink Floyd's classic segued into 'Where the Streets Have No Name' as Charlene replaced the handset and tidied the bar.

An hour later, I took a break and plopped on a stool.

"Could I fetch you a drink?" asked Charlene.

"Thanks, I'll have a light beer please."

Rick bumped the dining room door open and clonked empty glasses on the counter.

"What was that all about," I asked, "with the chap in the red shirt?"

"The one who bothered you on stage?" said Charlene. "He's a bloody troublemaker. He had too much to drink, turned rowdy and upset people. I called the cops, but by the time they answered, Rick had persuaded him to leave."

I glanced at Rick's biceps as he bent down to stack the dishwasher and figured someone he'd persuaded to leave wouldn't return any time soon.

≈ ≈ ≈

TAP TAP TAP

I rubbed my eyes and tugged my bedroom curtain back. Linda's face emerged through the condensation. I opened the window.

"There's a phone call for you," she said. "It's the police."

13. SMOOTH CRIMINAL

My upper cheeks tingled.

"The police? What do they want?"

"No idea. They didn't say."

I tugged on clothes and contemplated a selection of potential legal infractions. Jumping a red? Impossible, the West Coast had no traffic lights. Speeding? Maybe. Drunk driving? Definitely not; I always limited myself to one or two beers.

I sprinted to the farmhouse and picked up the receiver.

"Hello?"

A deep, ponderous voice. "Simon Michael Prior?"

"Yes?" I bit the inside of my cheek.

"Sergeant Tony McCulloch from Hokitika police. We need you at the station to answer a few questions. Could you come now, please?"

"Err, sure. I'll be there in thirty minutes."

I replaced the receiver and glanced at Linda.

"They need me to answer some questions at the police station."

She grinned at me. "Jeez, is your guitar playing that bad?"

≈ ≈ ≈

The modern, red-brick, single-storey Hokitika police station had a gentle ramp up to its glass door. I pulled my baseball cap over my eyes, nipped in and glanced around to make sure no-one I knew had observed me entering.

A young, stocky lady in police uniform stood on the opposite side of a glass partition. I took a deep breath and approached her.

"Err, hello. I'm here to see Sergeant Tony McCulloch."

I shuffled my feet and played two-finger piano on her counter.

"Wait there," she said. "I'll fetch him for you."

I jammed my hands into my pockets and attempted to prevent my legs from enacting a nervous dance as if I had an urgent need for the bathroom.

A side door opened, and a policeman with fair hair and a blonde moustache stepped out. "Simon? Tony McCulloch. Come this way, please."

We entered a room with four chairs, two on either side of a white Formica table. I glanced at the high, barred window in the opposite wall and then at the door. Another, taller man wearing a navy blue T-shirt and cargo pants tailed us. He carried a buff-coloured, A4-size folder.

"Sit down, please," said Tony. "This is Detective Mark Meehan, who's going to ask you some questions."

I sat down, bit my nails and tried to recall any useful episodes of *The Bill* which featured this scenario.

Which one's the good cop?

They pulled out the chairs opposite me. Tony rotated his and sat on it the wrong way around, with his legs apart and his arms resting on its back. Mark titled and dated the top page of a pad in slow, careful writing. I crossed and uncrossed my legs.

"Am I in trouble?"

"Not at all.." said Tony.

Okay, you're the good cop.

".. we just need help with our enquiries."

I rubbed my forehead, and recalled the BBC newscaster's phrase, 'helping police with their enquiries'.

Mark opened the buff folder, removed a photograph, spun it around and slid it across the table. "Do you recognise this man?"

I held the photo up in front of me and squinted at a face resembling the aftermath of the twelfth round in *Rocky IV*. "Not sure. He might be the man I saw at the Ocean View Backpackers on Saturday night. I think he's the troublemaker who the owner, Rick, persuaded to leave as he was drunk."

I looked at the policemen and laughed nervously. "I mean, the man was drunk. Not Rick."

The officers didn't appreciate my humour.

I stretched my arm out and rotated the picture left and right. "I'm fairly sure it's him, but in this photo, he appears to have been in a serious car accident."

Mark jotted on his pad. "Tell me what happened when you saw him."

I clasped my hands and leant forwards on my elbows. "I'm a rock guitarist. You might have seen my posters in pubs around town: London Musician Simon Michael Prior."

Mark and Tony glanced at each other and shrugged. "Nope," said Mark. "Anyway, go on."

"Rick employed me to perform music at the Ocean View Backpackers, and a drunk man joined me on stage and started singing into my microphone. He even tried to take my guitar from me and play it."

I waited while Mark scribbled more notes.

He tapped the top of the photo twice. "Is this the man you're referring to?"

"Yes. I'm sure it's him. I recognise his red shirt apart from anything."

I picked up the photo again and pursed my lips. "But when he bothered me, he looked in one piece. How did his face become smashed up so badly?"

Mark looked at Tony. Tony nodded once.

"Turns out our boy's a gold miner, down on his luck, drinking his sorrows," said Mark. "After Rick threw him out during your performance, this chap decided he didn't like Rick much. Following his eviction, our suspect visited his mining supplies and collected a stick of dynamite. He returned to the backpackers later when Rick and Charlene were clearing up, entered the rear door with the lit stick of dynamite and threatened to blow the place sky-high."

My eyes widened, and I looked at the photo again. "Wow. Did it go off in his face or something?"

"Fortunately not," said Mark. "If it had exploded, it would've killed them all. Rick managed to snatch the dynamite and throw it into a bucket of water he had for mopping the floor."

"Phew." I stared at the picture and tilted my head. "But that still doesn't explain why this guy looks so injured."

"You've seen the size of Rick?"

I nodded.

"This photo was taken after Rick had incapacitated him."

My eyebrows raised, and I placed the photo back on the table. Mark and Tony stood up.

"Once he's discharged from Greymouth hospital, we're charging our dynamite boy with attempted murder. I'll type up my notes; could you please pop in tomorrow and sign your statement?"

"Of course."

My knees shook as I pushed the chair in. I wasn't accustomed to police interviews about attempted murderers I'd sung duets with.

≈ ≈ ≈

"Where are you playing tonight?" asked Frank at dinner.

"The Brunner Working Men's Club. I rang them and spoke with a committee member. He said they only arrange one band per year so I'm honoured they've booked me."

"Gosh. I think the last time I entered there was for a meatworks function back in the 1960s. Be careful driving home. It's over an hour away and the temperature'll drop below freezing tonight."

"Thanks, Frank; I will."

My lights shone full beam to cut through the midwinter early nightfall. Layers of mist settled on the fields, and I caught glimpses of the werewolf-full moon. I swung a curve in the small town of Kaniere to dodge around several sheep who had broken through their fence and treated the asphalt as an electric blanket.

The barman of the Brunner Working Men's Club leant across the counter and conversed with the sole customer, an elderly man who wore an Emmenthal-holed jumper accessorised by fingerless gloves and a beanie hat that read *Waikato Milking Systems*. I glanced up to the rafters and noticed deflated pink balloons and paper streamers which had outlived long-forgotten shindigs.

The barman raised his eyebrows. "Can I help you? Are you a new member?"

The customer rotated on his stool and nodded at me.

"No, I'm the musician tonight. Simon Michael Prior."

The musician playing to an audience of one.

"Oh, yes, Wayne mentioned he'd booked you." He pointed to the other end of the empty hall. "Set up your gear on the stage. D'you want a drink?"

I rubbed my arms. "I don't suppose you could make me a cup of tea, please?"

He raised his eyebrows and sidled through a door behind the bar. I heard a kettle.

The customer sipped his beer and spoke slowly to me. "What music d'you play then?"

His red, puffy face hadn't seen the edge of a Gillette in decades.

"A bit of everything. From the '60s to the '90s. The Beatles to Oasis."

"Can you play anything old?"

I spoke louder. "Yes, The Rolling Stones, The Beatles, Elvis. My repertoire includes a lot of '60s music."

He waved the back of his hand at me twice. "They're not old. I can't stand all this modern rubbish. D'you play any Johnnie Ray?"

"Johnnie who?"

"Johnnie Ray. The American blues singer. What about Pat Boone? Big Joe Turner? I know; Gene Vincent. You must be able to play some Gene Vincent."

I shook my head slowly and shrugged. "Sorry, I'm not familiar with those artists."

His eyes took on an unfocussed gaze. "We used to hold the most wonderful dances here, y'know. Back in the day when music was music, I'd whirl my wife around this floor to Gene Vincent." He pressed his lips together and inspected his beer.

The barman returned and placed a chipped, white Ravensdown Fertiliser-logoed mug in front of me. I blew on the hot, stewed tea and slurped it. My insides defrosted a couple of degrees.

The customer finished his drink, pushed his glass towards the barman and stood. "I'll be seeing you, Grant."

He saluted me with his index finger. "Have a great night."

His back disappeared out of the door into the dark, and the barman picked up the empty glass and inserted it into a dishwasher. I now had an audience of precisely none.

"Right," I said. "I'll bring my gear in." I placed my unfinished tea on the bar.

My footsteps echoed on the bare wooden boards as I stepped out to my car, placed my hands on my hips and stared into the winter pitch-black. The moon had set, and my eyes failed to adjust to the night.

They're paying you three hundred dollars for this, Simon; you'd better give them a show. Even if no-one's here, and you've never heard of Gene Vincent.

I felt along the side of the car, opened the driver's door, flipped the seat up and reached into the rear of the car for my speakers. Once I'd carried them inside, I returned for my guitar and pulled it from the car boot. I made my last journey to fetch my bag of cables. The passenger door clicked open, and I ran my hands over the front seat to locate the holdall's handles. The hair on the back of my neck stood on end, and I froze.

An invisible something in the driver's seat exhaled.

14. EMPTY ROOMS

I strode back to the barman, who read a newspaper spread across the counter.

He furrowed his brow. "Everything all right?"

I glanced wide-eyed over my shoulder and pointed at the open door. "Are there wild animals around here?"

"Wild animals? Nope. What's wrong? You look like you've seen a ghost."

"I was bringing my gear in from my car, and something huge breathed on me in the dark."

The barman grinned and slapped his hand on the counter. "That'll be Brandy."

"Brandy?"

I had a vision of a living four-legged bottle of Remy Martin.

"Brandy. The old horse. He's tethered outside."

"Oh, right." I pressed my palm to my chest and let out a breath. "A horse."

The barman grinned, shook his head and recommenced his perusal of the sports page. I walked back outside, extracted Brandy's head from his inspection of my steering wheel and slammed the car doors.

The stage appeared ridiculously large for the evening's total absence of spectators. I sound-checked with a few bars of 'Hurts So Good', adjusted amplifier knobs and strummed a few random chords.

The barman coughed behind me. "Could you play quieter, please? They don't like it loud here."

I gazed across the empty hall and wondered who he referred to. "Sure." I tested a few bars at a lower volume to demonstrate.

The barman nodded at me and returned to his newspaper.

Eight o'clock. Time to begin the concert of the century.

I sang 'The Young Ones'.

To nobody.

The barman waved, and I paused mid-Cliff.

"Can you turn it down a bit?"

I drew in a deep breath and released it slowly. "Umm, okay."

This is ridiculous. Why am I here?

As I merged 'The Young Ones' into 'Summer Holiday', a middle-aged man entered the club, accompanied by a lady of similar vintage and a plain-looking woman in her twenties who could've been their daughter. I'd never been more pleased to perform to an audience of three people. They perched on stools at the bar. I finished my Cliff Richard medley, and the younger lady clapped, turned to her parents and said, "He's pretty good."

I grinned.

Wow, audience feedback. That's unexpected.

I began Elvis Presley's 'Jailhouse Rock'. The younger lady grabbed her mother's hand and pulled her into the centre of the hall. They commenced a jerky, awkward dance routine. The man paid the barman for three drinks.

Maybe this won't be such a terrible night. What can I play next to keep the atmosphere?

I completed Elvis, and the ladies clapped.

"Thank you very much," I said into my microphone as I started 'Live It Up' by Mental As Anything.

Wrong move. Too modern. The ladies returned to the bar and ignored me. I now had to stand on stage like an idiot and complete an upbeat song with no-one responding. The tune finished, and the ensuing silence was interrupted only by the small group conversing with the barman. I stared at the wooden boards of the stage.

Invisible musician: Simon Michael Prior.

The trio departed, and I performed once more to an empty space. The barman locked up the till and laid his keys on the counter.

I stopped playing and approached him. "D'you want me to carry on? There's no-one here."

"No point," he said. "Pack your stuff up."

He pulled an envelope from his pocket and handed it to me. I counted out six fifty-dollar notes.

"Thanks. I feel guilty taking it from you. You wouldn't have covered my cost tonight."

The barman folded his arms across his chest and shrugged. "Don't worry about it. The members are always nagging the committee to put on a band. We book one occasionally to prove to them no-one ever turns up. We could put The Beatles on, and none of them would come."

He turned around and flicked off light switches. I packed up my gear, said goodbye to Brandy the horse and drove away into the night.

≈ ≈ ≈

The embers of the living room fire glowed as orange as a West Coast sunset. Frank read the newspaper. Linda knitted. Fiona watched a repeat of *Fawlty Towers*. I glanced at the antics of Basil whacking Manuel with a tea-tray.

"It's a cold one tonight," said Linda. "D'you want a hot water bottle?"

My brow furrowed. "Hot water bottle? I don't think I've used one since my childhood."

"Thanks for reminding me, Mum," said Fiona. "I'll switch on the electric blanket."

She opened the kitchen door and vanished to our hut.

Frank lay the newspaper in his lap. "I'm driving to Christchurch tomorrow for a dinner. D'you want to come with me for the ride, Simon?"

"Sure. I don't have any gigs until Saturday."

"You can stay with me at the hotel. There'll be two beds in the room. I'm sure you can find something in the city to keep you occupied for the evening."

"You be careful crossing the pass in winter," said Linda. "Heavy rain's forecast. It'll be falling as snow up there."

Frank raised his eyebrows. "I think I'll manage. I've driven over it once or twice in my 64 years."

Linda turned to me. "You don't want to be stuck in Christchurch. Sometimes they close the pass for days."

"What d'you do if that happens?"

"We come home via the Lewis Pass, which adds another couple of hours, or we wait it out. Generally, we try not to traverse the mountains in winter."

Fiona returned from the hut. She hugged herself. "Brrr. It's freezing out there. Brrrr."

I frowned. "I can't work out why New Zealand houses aren't built with central heating."

"We don't really need it," said Linda.

My eyes widened as I felt the heat from the fire in the corner of the living room, and watched Fiona empty the kettle into a hot water bottle.

≈ ≈ ≈

I woke the following morning confused why I was sleeping in midwinter with no covers, and discovered a headless Fiona-shaped lump had stolen all the duvet and wrapped it around itself like a Swiss roll. I yanked on an edge and annexed a few rotations. A tug at the curtain revealed a vertical lake of condensation, which dripped down my arm and onto the bed as I polished a hole in it. I turned over, and a long-cold hot water bottle thudded on the floor.

"Seven o'clock, Fiona. Time to rise and shine for work."

"I want to stay in here forever," said the Swiss roll.

"I'll switch on the heater. This little hut won't take long to warm up."

I harvested a further square centimetre of covers, swung my legs out of bed and grabbed yesterday's clothes off the floor. I'd never dressed under a duvet before, but I worried I'd suffer frostbite in unusual places if I didn't. On the fourth *tic-tic-tic*, the gas heater ignited, and a blue flame glowed. My tea towel polished the condensation from the window and I gazed out at a white world, where frost caked every blade of grass as if a celestial baker had tripped over while carrying a Tupperware container of icing sugar.

The early morning sun reflected off miniature skating-rinks along both sides of the driveway and my bottom lip stuck out as Phillip's motorbike wheels spoiled the smooth, translucent puddle-ice.

Fiona stood beside me in her pyjamas, and we observed Frank busy with a hose. A bucket of water steamed on the ground as he rubbed his car with a cloth.

"It's going to be filthy again before we drive far," I said. "And his hands must be frozen."

"Dad always cleans his car before he goes away; it's one of his rituals. You'd better pack your bag."

"I'll be after you in the shower."

I watched Phillip load a bale of silage as I spooned in Nutri-grain. He hitched the tractor to the wagon and drove down the gravel track. The herd of cows pursued him along the fence line like children chasing the Mr Whippy van.

"Fiona, do the cows feel the cold?"

The shower water drummed as steam fogged from the bathroom.

"Pardon?" she said. "I can't hear you."

I dumped my bowl in the sink and stood next to the shower cubicle. "I said, do the cows feel the cold?"

"Of course they do; they're mammals, same as us."

"Poor cows. I'm glad we don't have to spend the night outside in this weather."

"Shall I leave the shower running?"

"Yes, please." I stripped off, and we high-fived as we exchanged places. She rubbed herself vigorously and wrapped a towel around her hair.

I dried myself and yanked on jeans and a jumper as Fiona stood beside the heater and tugged trousers on. "This reminds me of being a little girl getting ready for school in front of the fire."

"Will the hotel in Christchurch be this chilly?"

"You should pack a hot water bottle just in case."

I threw clean underwear into a bag, stuffed the hot water bottle on top and opened the door.

"Morning," I said to Frank. "I won't be long."

"Shut the door," said Fiona. "You're letting the heat out. D'you have a coat?"

"I'll be fine. See you tomorrow evening."

I kissed her and headed into the winter wonderland.

≈ ≈ ≈

Frank sped across icy puddles and swerved around frosty corners as we passed herds of cows feasting on steaming silage. The rising sun behind the mountains defined their peaks, and the snow blanketed them down to their foothills. I wondered what scene we'd find at the pass.

"How's the music going?" asked Frank.

"It's pretty quiet. The pubs aren't busy in winter. I'm playing at the Hokitika Chartered Club this weekend. D'you ever go there?"

Frank set his mouth in a straight line, and he rocked his head from side to side. "I haven't for a long time. It's a funny crowd; not the type of people I mix with. Have you tried looking for gigs elsewhere? North of Greymouth, there's another town called Westport. It'd be further to go, but if you obtained a booking for both the Friday and Saturday nights it'd be worth it."

"All right, I'll grab the phone book when we return home."

Frank switched on the radio. An AM station played rock n' roll music interspersed with horse racing commentary. I half-listened, and gazed at the lush, dripping scenery as the car sped through the foothills. I'd travelled this road several times now and knew what to expect at every turn; the jagged mountains, the impenetrable forests, the crashing waterfalls all entranced me. I remembered English journeys parked on the M25 motorway for the best part of a day and ruminated on how relaxed life had become.

Frank's version of sightseeing was slightly different, and he pointed out some interesting highlights as we careered around the curves.

"This bend here, it must have been in the mid-1960s, was where the Hokitika doctor ran off the road coming home after dark from Christchurch. He missed the turn and ended up over the bank. They didn't find his body until the next day."

I made the appropriate noises to note the passing of someone I'd never known who'd died before my birth. We crossed the single railway track carrying the daily milk and coal train over the mountains.

Frank pointed. "At this sharp curve in the road, years ago, Graham Francis died. His tyre had deflated, and the bloody idiot decided to change it right on the bend. A truck carting hay cleaned him up a few minutes later. Graham would never have known what hit him."

"That's terrible, Frank. Did you know him well?"

"Not really. Another farmer. He came from the Grey Valley."

The road crossed the river on a single-lane bridge. The route became steeper, and slush ridged on the verges.

"Then here, before the bridge, old Bert Hammond drove his truck over the edge into the river and killed himself. They never found out why. Some people say his brakes failed coming down the pass, but personally, I reckon he'd had a few too many whiskies."

"Was he a friend of yours?"

"My father knew him well. He must have been over ninety so he had a good innings. That happened back in the late '70s. The route's been improved since."

I studied the blind bends, single-lane bridges and waterfalls trickling over the road and wondered what state it must have been in at the time of Frank's reminiscences. We rounded a corner, and the road climbed towards the summit.

"Will the pass be open?" I asked.

"They would have turned us around by now if they'd closed it. But keep your eyes peeled for falling rock; all this recent rain will have loosened the ground."

We ascended through the single-lane section. The road clung to the side of the mountain, pinched between the cliff face on our left, and the river below us to the right. I glimpsed white water sluicing between garage-sized boulders. Frank slammed his hand on the steering wheel, and I jerked forwards against the seatbelt.

"Shit," he said, "look at that bloody thing."

15. ROCK AND ROLL DREAMS COME THROUGH

My eyebrows shot up and my mouth fell open as, in slow motion, a beach ball-sized rock pirouetted gracefully down the cliff face, smacked the road surface, split into two and hesitated. Frank skidded around the first section. He couldn't avoid the second, and a dull crunch and a grinding noise screeched from under the car.

"Bloody hell," he said. He stopped in the middle of the road, opened the driver's door, stepped out and bent down.

"It's stuck under the car. Can you give me a hand?"

He glanced up and down the road as sleet diagonalled through the car door.

I crouched on the asphalt and inspected the rock. "How do we pull it out?"

"Whatever we do," said Frank, "we have to be quick." He glanced up at the cliff face. "Something else might fall."

He tugged a wheel brace from the car boot, lay down and chipped at the rock with minimal effect.

"How about lifting up the car?" I asked.

"Good idea." Frank grabbed a car jack from the boot and wound the end.

A distant engine noise reverberated around the valley.

"Frank, TransWest Freighter's coming. He needs to maintain momentum to climb the pass."

The car wheel lifted off the road surface.

"Simon, see if you can pull it out."

I lay down on the road and heaved at the rock. The approaching truck's engine's pitch rose in steps as it changed down through the gears. "It's not budging."

Frank glanced in the direction of the approaching truck. "Kick it."

I kicked it. "I think it moved."

Sweat ran over my face and merged with the falling sleet.

"Stand back," said Frank. He reached under the car with both hands, grabbed the rock and jerked his whole body. With a metal scraping sound, the rock popped out, and he shoved it over the edge into the river.

I wound down the jack, flung it in the boot and hopped in the passenger seat. Frank sat down heavily, slammed his door and accelerated.

The truck followed metres behind us. Frank checked the rear-view mirror and brushed dirt off his coat. He glanced at me. "I don't suppose that eventuates too often on the motorway in England."

≈ ≈ ≈

We summitted the pass and headed into the flat, straight roads of the Canterbury Plains. Frank's horse racing radio station didn't hold my interest, and I dozed. At one point, I opened my eyes as Frank sped up furiously on the wrong side of the road to overtake a truck while another truck bore down on us. I decided the safest course of action was to close my eyes again.

The last daylight disappeared, and the smell of wood smoke permeated through the air vents as we pulled up outside a single-storey hotel. I rubbed my eyes, stretched and yawned.

"I'll check in," said Frank. "There'll be two beds in the room but the booking's for one person, so don't be too obvious."

"All right, I'll wait behind the pillars."

An easel outside a large conference room displayed an aerial view of circular tables, with names listed beside them, and a menu. I imagined myself at the meal and chose the beef carpaccio followed by the roast rack of lamb. My mouth watered at the prospect of sticky date pudding with vanilla ice cream, when Frank tapped my shoulder and dangled a key.

"Ready? They couldn't find my reservation, but I stay here regularly so they gave me a room."

We trooped along a mile-long corridor with red and yellow diamond-patterned carpet. Repetitive wall-prints fixed at regular intervals displayed various views of New Zealand's stunning scenery. The passage turned a sharp right, and an identical corridor stretched into the distance like one of the more disturbing scenes from *The Shining*. Frank inserted the key into one of hundreds of indistinguishable doors. He propped it open for me, and I entered the standard hotel room configuration.

Bathroom on the right.

Wardrobe on the left.

Bed straight ahead.

Bed. One bed.

"Err, Frank, I think we have a problem."

Frank followed me into the room and raised his eyebrows. "Oh, I thought every room in this hotel had two beds."

"Now what? We can't complain to reception; I'm not supposed to be here."

"We'll have to share the bed."

"Really?"

Frank winked. "I'm joking. The manager knows me; I'll find him. Wait here."

I sat on the end of the bed then stood up and smoothed the depression made by my bottom. The hotel information folder depicted Hollywood-opulent swimming pools and tennis courts, none of which would be open at this time of year.

Frank entered and dangled another key. "Ready to change address?"

I grabbed the bags and pursued him along the corridor to a different room.

Bathroom on the right.

Wardrobe on the left.

Beds straight ahead.

Beds.

Two double beds.

I dumped my bag on the left-hand bed and unpacked. Frank hung up his tuxedo.

He extracted a folder from his briefcase, laid it on the dresser, opened it and ran his finger down a page. He paused, glanced back at the top of the sheet and turned to me.

"Did you unpack already?"

"I did."

"Ah. Can you fold it all up again? It's no wonder they couldn't find my booking. We're at the wrong hotel."

≈ ≈ ≈

We repeated the process at the Wyndham, and Frank departed for his dinner. I perched on the edge of my bed.

What am I going to do tonight? I can't sit in the room all evening by myself.

I flicked through a brochure entitled 'Things to do in Christchurch: The Garden City.' Among glossy colour images of museums, gardens and art galleries hid a small advertisement for a venue called The Christchurch Cavern. It announced: Live Music: every Thursday to Sunday.

Time to study the competition.

I threw on a denim jacket, grabbed the spare room key and clicked the door behind me.

A shuttle bus disgorged passengers at the hotel entrance. The driver's shorts and socks recklessly disregarded the season, and on his top he wore a hotel-logoed jacket. He heaved suitcases from the rear of the bus, and guests trundled them into reception. I hesitated until the last bag had been claimed, and he'd closed the boot.

"Are you waiting for a ride to the airport?" he asked. He pulled his hood back to reveal white hair and rubbed his hands.

"No, but could you drive me to the city? Is it far?"

"It's fifteen minutes away. I can take you there, assuming you're a guest."

"I'm staying in the hotel tonight."

This wasn't strictly a lie.

The bus's headlights pierced the wood smoke-haze as we headed into Christchurch city centre. I couldn't comprehend how the driver could see the road ahead. Reds and greens of traffic lights blurred towards us then dissolved instantly, and the faint headlight of a brave cyclist waited at a road junction. The bus dropped me close to Cathedral Square. Swirls of smog prevented me from seeing the other side of the street, and I expected a top-hatted Colin Firth to arrive in a hansom cab at any point.

The Christchurch Cavern stood camouflaged in a back street behind the square. Dark material concealed all the windows, and dim blue and green lights illuminated the interior. Midnight-coloured paint must have been on special offer when the business decided their interior design, as the proprietors had painted every surface black, from the walls and bar to the tall tables scattered around the perimeter. My eyes became drawn to the carpet pattern, which consisted entirely of cigarette burns and splotchy stains, and the essence of stale smoke and ingrained body odour saturated the air. A fat man in a denim waistcoat stacked bottles into a fridge, and a short, skinny chap wearing tight leather trousers and a black T-shirt carried amplification gear from a side door.

He set down a speaker with the words 'The Gear Junkies' stencilled on the side in white writing and leant against it.

I approached him. "Hi, are you the band tonight?"

His long, blonde hair flicked back, spraying a shower of sweat liberally around the room like a golden retriever after a swim. "I'm their manager." He grinned and rolled his eyes. "And their roadie by the looks of it. The lazy bastards have gone to eat a burger and left me to it. Same as every night."

He grinned and held out a hand. "I'm Cage."

I took it then subtly wiped my palm on my jeans. "I'm Simon, a musician from Hokitika. Well, London, originally, but I've been gigging the West Coast pubs for a few months."

He extracted a packet of cigarettes from his back pocket and flipped it open in my direction. I declined.

"Hokitika, hey? We headlined the Wild Foods Festival there in March. Did you play? Great gig."

He stuffed a Marlboro in his mouth and struck a match on his shoe in a well-rehearsed move.

"I wasn't playing at the festival," I said. "I visited as a paying customer, but I ate a Huhu grub and felt ill so I returned home."

Cage chuckled. "Yep, they eat some funny things on the Coast. You should ask for a spot at the festival next year. There's a bloke who organises it; I think he's called Mike. Why not pay him a call?"

"Do they employ solo musicians as well as bands?"

"You don't know until you ask."

Cage hoisted an amplifier on top of the speaker. It slid off, and I grabbed one edge.

"D'you need a hand with the gear?"

"Only if you've nothing to do. I'd appreciate it."

He patted my back, and we exited to his van.

≈ ≈ ≈

Cage and I sat on the edge of the stage. I idly twanged an unplugged guitar and looked up as four men crashed through the side door.

"G'day, Cage," said the tallest one. He flicked his long, peroxide hair out of his eyes. "Who's ya mate?"

"This is Simon," said Cage. "He's a solo musician who plays pubs around Hokitika."

He pointed to the four band members. "Simon, this is Steve, our singer, Tim, on guitar, Jus, the bass player and Rocky, who bangs the drums."

These guys had exactly modelled their appearance on the big hair of Bon Jovi.

"We know Hokitika," said Steve. "We performed there in March."

"Have you played Wild Foods?" asked Tim.

"Great gig," said Jus.

"I didn't this year," I said, "but I hope to in 1998."

Rocky pointed at Cage. "D'you know why they call him Cage?"

"Nope. Why?"

"'Cos the runt's so bloody skinny, you can see his rib cage."

The four dissolved into laughter. I reckoned Cage took a lot of stick from them.

Steve turned to me. "D'you want to join us on stage for a couple of numbers tonight?"

"Great idea," said Tim. He stretched out his thumbs and index fingers and drew an imaginary banner in the air. "Guest artist, Simon, all the way from Hokitika."

They all laughed again.

"I'm from London, originally," I said.

Tim repeated the gesture. "International guest artist, Simon, all the way from Hokitika."

More laughter. I wondered how many beers they'd drunk with the burgers.

"Here's the song list," said Jus. He handed me a dog-eared piece of card covered in sticky tape.

I ran my finger down it. "I know most of these. How d'you go with 'Living Next Door to Alice'?"

"Crowd participation song," said Rocky. "We'd never escape alive if we didn't perform that."

"Okay. What about 'Summer of '69'?"

"Sounds good," said Tim. "You can play lead. I'll take a break."

I gave them a huge grin and nodded.

"We'd better prepare for showtime," said Steve. He turned to Cage. "Is everything ready in the stars' dressing room?"

Cage blew a raspberry. "Stars' dressing room? D'you mean the gents' toilets?"

We all laughed, and the band members headed for a door at the rear. I patted Cage's shoulder, led him to the bar and bought him a beer. I reckoned he needed one.

≈ ≈ ≈

Within an hour, the venue filled with denim-jacketed long-haired men and pale-faced girls with tiny leather skirts and black make-up. I leant against the bar, watched Cage tune Tim's instrument and tapped my foot to 'The Final Countdown' which blasted from ceiling speakers. Cage stepped down and clinked glasses with me.

The background music truncated mid-chorus as two white spotlights shone on the stage, and dry-ice smoke covered the floor, randomly reminding me of West Coast winter mist. The four musicians materialised, having consumed 34 cans of hair spray and 20 kilos of black mascara between them.

A deep voice sounded from overhead.

"And now.."

Pause.

"Ladies and gentlemen.."

Pause.

"Please give it up for tonight's band: The Gear Junkies."

Tim struck the opening riff of 'Sweet Child o' Mine.'

This is how it should be. No Kenny Rogers and Cliff Richard. No gentle instrumentals while people finish sodding apple crumbles. Straight into the good stuff.

I grinned, clapped my hands above my head and tapped my foot.

'Love in an Elevator' followed, then 'Sweet Home Alabama'.

Cage smiled and gave me two thumbs up. He bought us both another beer, touched his glass against mine again and I mouthed, "thanks."

Rock anthem followed rock anthem followed rock anthem. Hands waved, fists pumped the air, hoarse voices sang along. I sang along too. I couldn't help myself. 'Any Way You Want It' ended, and the lights dimmed except for a single spotlight. Tim stood in its beam while the other band members retreated into the shadows. He looked down at his guitar so his hair hid his face while he plucked the riff to 'Hotel California'.

He paused at the start of verse one, raised his head and silently conducted with his upturned palms. In unison, the crowd sang *a capella*. Cigarette lighters waved back and forth. The entire audience had eyes for the centre-stage man with the guitar.

I watched with my mouth open wide. The second verse finished, Rocky crescendoed the drums, Jus thumped the bass and Steve pointed his microphone out into the crowd as the band accompanied them in the chorus.

That's how you do it. I wish my gigs ran like this.

'Hotel California' ended, and the cheering and clapping lasted for several minutes.

Steve slid his microphone into its holder and spoke. "And now, a special guest artist. All the way from London: Simon Michael Prior."

Cage grinned and slapped me on the back. I turned to him, clenched my teeth and slid my eyes sideways.

How the hell will I follow that performance?

My legs didn't seem to function properly as I climbed the three steps to the stage. Tim handed me his guitar, and I spent a minute adjusting the strap to accommodate the difference in our heights. The audience cheered and shouted as if Eric Clapton himself had walked on. I shielded my eyes from the spotlights and glanced over at Cage, who stood at the bar with Tim.

Not only Tim.

Cage stood with Tim and Steve.

They stared back at me, raised beers and grinned.

Shit. I'm the guitarist and the singer?

I glanced over my shoulder and Jus gave me a thumbs up.

This is it. Here we go, Mister International Guest Artist all the way from Hokitika.

I started the familiar riff of 'Summer of '69'. My hands shook, and I worried I'd drop the plectrum. The words of the Bryan Adams classic blasted out from speakers behind me. I figured I'd better not stop singing in case the voice in the speakers stopped too. The audience nodded in time and joined in with the chorus. Cage, Steve and Tim saluted in my direction. As the song finished, I raised my fist in the air, bowed and waited for the applause to die down.

Yes! I'm a rock legend.

I smiled behind the microphone and sang the first line to 'Living Next Door to Alice'. At the appropriate point, I paused and cupped one hand to my ear as the crowd added the alternative refrain, complete with the profanities. Multiple choruses later, Tim ascended the steps and made it clear he wanted his guitar back. Steve grabbed the microphone and thrust his left arm out straight.

"Ladies and gentlemen, Simon Michael Prior."

I lifted my arms high in the air and exited stage left as the band smashed out Kiss's 'Crazy Crazy Nights' behind me. Cage waited at the bar. We high-fived, and I threw my head back with my eyes closed and exhaled.

"Hey, Simon, you were fantastic," he said. "Make sure you come and say hello at the Wild Foods Festival. You could perform with us again."

"I will, thanks, Cage. Erm, what time is it?"

"I've no idea. Oh, there's a clock behind the bar. Quarter to midnight."

"Wow. I'd better go. Good to meet you."

We shook hands, and I jostled through the crowd to the pub door. A row of taxis waited at a rank, and I jumped in the first one, sagged back and pushed my head against the seat. A warm glow permeated through my whole body.

I've just had the best experience of my life.

I'm a rock star.

I'm London Musician Simon Michael Prior.

The taxi driver coughed politely and addressed me through his thick, black beard.

"Where to, sir?"

His yellow turban scraped against the roof.

"Err, my hotel, please."

"Which hotel, sir?"

I bit my lip and glanced left and right. "Um, I can't remember."

16. DON'T STOP ME NOW

The taxi driver smiled. Clearly, this wasn't the first time a slightly drunk international guest artist from Hokitika had materialised in his cab with no idea of where he wanted to be taken.

"Can you remember what your hotel looks like, sir?"

"It's big. Miles and miles of corridors."

"How many storeys does it have, sir?"

"One. It only has a ground floor."

"It must be a hotel near the airport, sir. Is it The Commodore?"

"Nope."

He pulled away from the kerb and drove slowly. "The Skylodge?"

"Nope."

"The Travel Inn?"

"I don't think so."

We passed an advertisement. I cupped my chin in my hand, then pointed. "There. In the picture. That's my hotel."

"Very good, sir. Taking you to The Wyndham."

Fifteen minutes later, the taxi entered the semicircular hotel driveway.

"Thirteen dollars please, sir."

I undid the seatbelt, squirmed in my pocket and pulled out my room key. Gold embossed print on a white background glared 'The Wyndham' at me from the tag.

The taxi driver grinned and held up one finger. "Next time you forget which hotel you are staying at, sir, I recommend you look in your pocket."

≈ ≈ ≈

Heavy rain drumming on the window woke me. I turned over, observed Frank's bed empty and heard the shower running. As the toilet resided in the bathroom, and my bladder had expanded to the size of a hot-air balloon, this scenario was going to cause me a formidable issue. I attempted to dress while crossing my legs and exited into the corridor to track down alternative arrangements. The smell of bacon attracted me to breakfast, and I hoped Frank's room rate included it, although I wasn't sure if we'd both be able to sneak a full English. Drips of rain blew through the open window in the main toilets and brought with them the unmistakable smell of wet plants. My mind recalled the events of the previous evening.

The stage.

The crowd.

The atmosphere.

This is what I'm meant to do. I want more nights like that.

I breathed out and returned to the bedroom.

Frank closed his suitcase and zipped a cover around his tuxedo.

"I popped out to the toilet," I said. "Breakfast smells good." I raised my eyebrows at Frank.

"Mine's included," he said. "I'll tell them I've brought a guest. It'll be okay."

≈ ≈ ≈

Hotel patrons milled around buffet tables containing hot food, pastries and fruit. A young girl in a white top and black skirt waltzed through the diners, topping up coffees and clearing empty plates. Frank and I sat with full cooked breakfasts, which formed a much-needed beer sponge in my case.

"How was your dinner?" I asked.

"The usual. Boring speeches, chicken or beef depending on who you sat next to and continual top-ups of Pinot Noir. Where d'you end up last night?"

"A live music venue called the Christchurch Cavern. I met a band there and smashed out a couple of numbers with them on stage. They encouraged me to apply for the Wild Foods Festival."

"Have you been to see Mike Keenan yet?"

"I will do, soon. I want to perform a few more gigs first. If I can play anywhere similar to last night, I'm sure he'll be impressed."

≈ ≈ ≈

The Hokitika Chartered Club's barman washed glasses in a small counter-top machine as I strolled across the room. "Hi. I'm Simon Michael Prior, the entertainment for tonight."

"Oh, right. I'm Andy. Set yourself up over there. D'you want anything to eat or drink?"

His physical build and polite but firm demeanour made me wonder if he'd been a rugby full-back in his youth.

"A lemonade, thanks."

I brought my gear in from my car and glanced around the room as I assembled it. A carpet in the style of 1970s headmaster's study offset the bare, white walls. Two elderly couples dined in the opposite corner, and a group of five middle-aged men sat at a circular, metal-legged table which displayed a vast assortment of empty glasses in the centre. The men added to this collection frequently, and I concluded they'd been there all afternoon.

This would be a background music event.

I opened with Crowded House's 'Distant Sun'. A laid-back, relaxed number and a New Zealand band too. As I plucked the intro, I approached the microphone. "Good evening, everyone. I'm London Musician Simon Michael Prior, and I'll be entertaining you tonight."

An obese man in the group of five stood up, glanced in my direction and waddled to the bar. His tummy peeked from the bottom of his shirt, which displayed a series of food-stain medals. No-one else took any notice of my performance which suited me fine. This crowd weren't exactly about to jump up and start jiving.

I paused between songs and sipped from my lemonade. The conversation among the group at the circular table continued in a loud and animated fashion. The men waved their arms, thumped the surface and discussed absent acquaintances. They didn't seem to have a high opinion of them.

As I crooned the acoustic version of 'Layla', I heard the fat man lean back on two legs of his chair and refer to 'the pommy prick who can't sing'.

I blinked rapidly, shook my head and almost stopped mid-Clapton. He conversed with his fellow drunkards and didn't look my way.

'Layla' ended. Nobody clapped or acknowledged me. I played more numbers and decided I'd imagined the man's insults.

At my first break, I asked for a second lemonade. The fat man walked up to the bar, stood next to me and pulled out his wallet.

"Another round, please, Andy," he said to the barman. He didn't glance at me or interact in any way. I'd definitely mis-heard his comment. I returned to my guitar and played the opening chords of 'Brown Sugar'. The older couples had departed, and the group in the centre remained the sole customers. I decided it didn't matter what I played; the night was a write-off. The fat man pushed himself up with some difficulty. He held onto his chair to prevent himself from toppling sideways and jabbed his finger at me.

"Now you think you're bloody Mick Jagger, d'you? You can't sing, and you can't play, you pommy tosser."

I stepped back and avoided looking at him.

One of his accomplices tugged his arm. "Leave it, Dennis, he's not worth it."

Dennis stuck two fingers up, sneered and sat down heavily on a chair I was becoming increasingly optimistic could no longer hold his weight.

Andy the barman hadn't noticed Dennis's outburst. I continued playing and convinced myself I heard him make further derogatory comments, but my ears may have been playing tricks.

I started Tom Petty's 'I Won't Back Down'.

Dennis stood up, wobbled and jabbed his finger. "You're a bloody useless pom, that's what you are." He leant heavily on one side of the table, and I secretly hoped it would tip over and he'd land on his face.

His friends also rose. They nodded at the barman and staggered out. Dennis gave me another rude gesture as he exited. I played to the end of the song and approached Andy, as he made several journeys to the round table, ferrying empty glasses to the bar. I wondered if he'd completely run out of pints.

"Bit quiet tonight?" I said.

"Yep. You may as well finish up. There won't be anyone else in. It's always empty in winter."

I looked at him to gauge if he'd be on my side and decided to risk it. "That group of men sitting here. They, erm, seemed to be enjoying a good night. D'you know them?"

Andy wiped the table and nodded.

"Dennis Stark and his colleagues? They're probably my best customers. They keep the place going."

Dennis Stark. How do I know that name?

"Oh right. Are they farmers, or fishermen? What do they do?"

"Some of them are farmers. Mostly, they own local businesses. But they've one thing in common. They're all members of the council."

≈ ≈ ≈

We watched the evening news after dinner the next day. Fiona and I sat beside each other and shared a blanket. Frank sipped a mug of tea, folded the *Christchurch Press* to an inner page and studied the weekend's racing form.

Linda removed her glasses and discarded her knitting. "I'd better check on number 132. She was standing away from the herd this afternoon, and I reckon she's about to drop."

"Drop?" I said. "D'you mean she's going to die?"

Linda laughed. "She's about to calve. Give birth. She'll be the first this spring. Once calving starts properly, we won't have time to think. D'you want to come with me and see if she's had it yet?"

I jumped up. "Of course. Let's go."

I might be able to help her and become a dad.

"It's a chilly night," said Frank. "Put on some warm clothes. And take my big torch."

≈ ≈ ≈

My breath formed clouds of steam as I waited for Linda in the farmhouse porch. I glanced up at a starless, moonless sky as black as Morticia Addams' fingernail varnish. Linda dressed in a farm coat and a thick woolly hat.

I searched around for Jazz. "Where's the dog?"

"Have a look in the washhouse."

I poked my nose around the laundry door and observed a nose and eyes poking out from under a pile of farm coats. Jazz lifted his eyebrows and queried me.

"He's pulled the jackets off the hangers to keep warm," I said.

"Yep," said Linda. "Sensible dog. He's not interested in stomping around fields in the dark."

I followed the sound of Linda's footsteps closely, terrified if I lost her I'd be abandoned in a field and never find my way home. I knew we'd reached the driveway when I heard the creak of the gate at the end of the path and the scrunch of her boots on the gravel. We trudged down an invisible track into the night.

"Here we are," said Linda's voice. I heard a paddock's latch and the squeak of an un-oiled gate.

Linda shut it behind us and reattached the chain. We walked into the field. Despite the cold weather, sweat formed on the inside of my clothes and I suppressed a strong desire to turn back.

I couldn't see the cows.

I couldn't hear the cows.

But I could sense the cows.

I'd no idea how this could be possible, but I could feel the presence of two hundred cows.

My gaze darted around in the darkness. "Linda, where are you?"

"Here. What are you scared of? They're the same cows you milk and feed every day."

"Yes, but in the dark, they seem..bigger."

I heard a snort to my left, and my entire body trembled.

"Come on," said Linda. "I want to go back inside. It's freezing out here."

"What if we walk into a cow?"

"Oh, for goodness' sake. I'll turn the torch on."

I blinked several times as the beam played across placid animals standing up and staring at us or lying down and staring at us.

"Can you see number 132?" asked Linda. She walked among the cows, shining the torch on their left ears at the yellow identity tags. I remained in the torch beam, checking numbers. I thought I'd found her but I'd mistaken her for number 32.

"Here," said Linda.

I joined her next to one of the black-and-whites.

"She's had it," said Linda.

I rubbed my beanie hat. "Sorry?"

"She's had the calf. She's given birth. You can tell by looking at her." Linda shone the torch on the cow. I couldn't see any difference between her and all the others.

"Where's the calf?" I asked. "I'd expect it to be with its mother."

"Exactly. Where's the calf?"

I followed the circle of torchlight on the ground.

"She's a first-time mum so she'll have no experience with feeding a baby," said Linda. "Not all of them have maternal instincts."

Linda's torch beam swept from side to side. She shone it further into the distance and lit up the fence posts and wires at the field's edge.

I paused. "Back there. Shine your torch on that post. Near the base."

We marched towards the fence. A lump of something had caught my eye.

"Good spot. Here's where she put it."

Linda stood over the calf. It lay down with its legs spread, a miniature version of its mother and all its aunties. She crouched and placed her hand on it.

"Sorry, Simon. We're too late. It's dead."

17. NEW KID IN TOWN

A lump formed in my throat.

"Dead? But it's just been born."

"Number 132 didn't know how to feed her calf. Damn, I should have checked earlier. We might have saved it."

The tiny, black face lay in the torchlight. I studied its small body, its four little brown hooves, and thought about how it would never grow up to be a dairy cow, never know how the lush, green grass of New Zealand's West Coast tasted, never run through the paddocks with its herd.

Linda shone the torch at me. "Why are you looking upset? Once calving season's in full swing, you'll see plenty more dead animals. You won't have time to feel sad."

We trudged back to the farmhouse in silence.

≈ ≈ ≈

The spring rain paused for a lunch break, and pillows of assorted shades of grey scudded across the sky. Occasional pale blue patches peeked through holes in the clouds. Frank placed a small plate of Wattie's baked bean-saturated toast on the table, sat down and opened yesterday's paper.

The fire crackled in the living room.

"Calving time's the busiest period on the farm, isn't it?" I asked.

"Yep, we'll be flat out in a few days," said Frank.

He forked baked beans and turned the page of the paper.

My arm raised as if I were a school pupil. "What can I do to help? I'm at a loose end between music engagements. Can you assign me a task I'm responsible for?"

"I'll tell you what you can do," said Linda. "You can help me feed those bloody calves. I've fed them every spring, for decades, and I'm over it."

I sat at the edge of my chair, grinned and nodded. "I'd love to. It sounds fun, feeding baby animals."

"Seeing as you're so enthusiastic," said Linda, "there are a couple of cows who gave birth last night. You can help me separate them from the herd and bring them in, and we'll check if any others are close to delivery."

Maybe I can assist one and become a dad?

"Can I bring my camera? Do we transfer them to a nursery? A place where they can feed their babies in peace?"

Linda chuckled. "They don't feed their babies. We do. We separate the calves from their mothers, the cows enter the milking shed, and we give their babies milk from bottles."

I tried to process this piece of information. "That seems unnecessarily complicated. We lead the mothers into the milking shed, we milk them and we give the milk to the babies? Why don't we let the mothers feed them directly and cut out the shed bit?"

Frank laughed. "Sorry, Simon," He wiped his mouth with a paper towel. "Let me explain. The cows give about fifty litres of milk a day, of which the calves drink about four. The other forty-six goes in the vat, and the tanker collects it and takes it to the Westland Dairy factory."

"Ahh, now I understand."

"Plus, if any cows suffer from mastitis, their milk can't go in the vat because of the antibiotics."

"Yep, I recall when I made that mistake and nearly poisoned the day's supply."

"But the calves can drink it. It doesn't cause them any harm."

≈ ≈ ≈

Linda motored the four-wheel bike along the track while I perched on the mudguard. As we arrived at the paddock, I noticed two cows isolated from the main herd, each with a Great Dane-sized baby head-butting and nuzzling at its udder.

I paused and watched the magic of newborn animals finding their way in an unfamiliar, exciting world.

"Here we are," said Linda. "Two of them." She shaded her eyes and inspected the herd. "And here's another about to give birth." She pointed.

A cow stood by herself, with unexpected legs and hooves poking out of her rear. I bounced on my toes.

"Wow. Does she need any help? Can we wait, and watch her have the calf? I've never seen a baby cow being born."

I glanced up at the sound of a motorbike as Phillip arrived.

He kicked the bike's stand into position, vaulted the fence and pointed at the cow with the extra legs. "She's been in that position since last night. She's having trouble passing the calf. We'll have to give her a hand."

"Gosh," I said. "Are you going to perform a caesarean or something?"

Phillip laughed. "Nothing so drastic, thank goodness. I'm no surgeon."

He pulled two metal rods out of the four-wheel bike's bucket, each about a foot long, then unravelled blue twine and tied it around the rods so they formed a cross-shape. I watched and slid my camera out of my pocket. Phillip approached the two little legs sticking out of the cow's rear. He tied the other end of the twine around them and gave it a test tug. I held the camera to my eye. David Attenborough wouldn't have been any less attentive.

Phillip yanked at the twine. The legs became longer. He leant back and strained. A little body appeared, inside a thin, transparent sack which reminded me of a child blowing bubble gum. The cow didn't seem concerned someone was extracting a miniature version of herself from her back end. Phillip straightened his body, leant again and engaged in another sustained tug. An elongated, black sausage extruded from the cow. The bubble gum burst, and four legs and a body plopped onto the grass. Phillip removed the twine and pulled away the gum.

The calf didn't move.

I walked towards it, then paused. "Linda, it's not dead, is it? It's not another dead one?"

"Why are you whispering? It takes a minute for them to come around. Here we go."

The calf lifted its tiny head.

I grinned and hugged Linda, who stepped back and gave me an odd look.

"It's alive," I said. I raised my arms above my head and clapped. "We've got a live one."

The cow walked over to its newborn and licked it.

"C'mon," said Linda. "Let's bring these other two into the shed. We'll leave the new one until tomorrow."

Linda opened the rear of a cage fixed to the little trailer while Phillip picked up a day-old calf the size of a small pony. The calf immediately complained about this intrusion louder than a spoilt child in Pizza Hut. I poked my fingers in my ears to block out the bleating noise. The mother mooed urgently and continually without taking breaths. Linda started the four-wheel bike.

"Quick, Phillip," she said. "Shove the other calf in before this one escapes."

Phillip lifted the second baby and the bleating and mooing noises instantly duplicated. The mother objected to her calf being stolen and butted Phillip in the backside. She chased him around the side of the trailer, nudging him with her nose. Phillip sprinted past the front of the bike with the bleating black infant in his arms. They circumnavigated a second time, and *The Benny Hill Show* theme played in my head as Phillip reached the rear of the trailer again.

"Simon, open the bloody cage."

"I would if I could stop laughing."

I restrained the first mooing calf while Phillip completed another lap. He stuffed the calf into the trailer, clanged the cage shut and puffed with his hands on his knees. "Jeez, if I'd had to sprint another round, I would've passed you the baton."

Linda trundled the four-wheel bike towards the sheds, the bleating sound following her from the trailer. The cows weren't ecstatic that their calves had been abducted, and they trotted behind, mooing raucously. I nipped ahead and snapped a quick photo. This entire process of removing babies from their mothers directly after their birth unsettled me, but here we were on a dairy farm where daily life comprised such events.

Linda arrived at the shed, opened the trailer, and the calves jumped out. She clutched an oversized bottle of milk with a black teat on its top and stuffed it in the first calf's mouth. The bleating sound ceased instantly.

"Simon, grab that bottle and do the other one."

I copied her actions, picked up the white container and shoved the teat in. The calf sucked noisily and spilt milk over the hay. Phillip ushered the mothers into the milking shed.

"Linda," I called over the sound of slobbering, "what happens when there are more than two mouths to feed? I can only do one at a time."

Linda unplugged her calf. "We have a big bucket contraption with loads of teats. I'll show you later. Hey, your calf's finished. She's inhaling fresh air."

I wrestled the bottle from the calf's mouth. "Will these two grow up to be dairy cows?"

"All the girl calves will become part of the herd eventually."

"What about the boy calves?"

Linda drew her mouth in a straight line. "I'll break the news to you about them later. I don't want to upset you."

I wasn't sure what she meant, but my calf had reattached itself to the empty bottle and sucked like it had reached the end of a McDonald's cola, so I pulled its head and heaved it off the teat.

≈ ≈ ≈

Fiona unscrewed the lid from a bottle of cheap pinot noir while I cooked fajitas and rice. The gas fire popped and spluttered in the corner, and the smell of frying mince rose from the stove.

"This reminds me of when we lived in London," she said. "Every Saturday evening, you'd cook a meal, and we'd share a bottle of wine and discuss our travel plans." She sat down, stuck out her bottom lip and smoothed the tablecloth. "I miss those days in London. There are so many things I regret we didn't do, so many places we could have visited when we lived so close to them, and now we don't, and we can't."

She looked up at me, and her eyes glistened. "D'you think we'll live there again?"

"How can we? I mean, you're not legally allowed to live in Britain. Don't you enjoy being in New Zealand with your family?"

I placed two plates on the tiny dining table and sat opposite her. She forked some rice and pushed it into her mouth. I heard crunching.

"What's this?" she asked. "Rice is normally soft."

Oh no. I didn't boil it for long enough.

"Err, it's Mexican crunchy rice. My own recipe. What d'you think?"

Fiona crunched some more. She licked her lips. "It's yummy. You can make it again any time."

I smiled and cut the end from a fajita.

"I am enjoying living here," said Fiona. "New Zealand will always be home, but we might have to relocate to a city at some point. I mean, your guitar playing's a great hobby, but you'll have to return to reality one day; the once-a-week money doesn't exactly allow us to.."

The door to the hut flew open and Linda grasped the frame with her hand on her chest. "Quick, come to the farmhouse. Have you seen the news? Oh, my goodness."

18. TRAGEDY

"Quick," said Linda. She beckoned with her entire arm. "On the television."

"What?" said Fiona, as she pushed back her chair and stood. "What's happened?"

Linda swallowed hard. "It's Princess Diana. She's dead."

Fiona poked out her bottom lip, shook her head and shrugged. "She can't be. She's only about 35."

Linda beckoned again. "Frank was looking at horse racing results on teletext when he saw a line about a terrible car crash in Paris. It said Diana and Dodi have both been killed."

Fiona and I stared at each other with raised eyebrows and ran after Linda into the farmhouse.

Frank perched on the edge of the sofa and scrolled through orange text on the television screen. He pressed a button on the remote control, and the image changed to a newscaster dressed in a black suit, white shirt and black tie. A dated photo of Princess Diana receiving flowers from a small child displayed behind his left shoulder.

"Shocking news this morning from Europe, where details are emerging of a fatal car accident which has claimed the lives of Britain's Princess Diana and her partner, Dodi, the son of Harrod's owner Mohammed Al Fayed. We now cross to London where we link to the British Independent Television News for more details."

Fiona covered her mouth with one hand. I hadn't seen the Big Ben backdrop of England's ITN since the previous year and I didn't recognise the young night-time presenter. Early this London morning, anchorman Trevor McDonald might not yet have arisen, and the forthcoming media tsunami was about to spoil his Weetabix.

"Good morning. The Press Association issued a newsflash at 4.41 a.m. to state Diana, Princess of Wales, has died in a car accident in Paris. Her partner, Dodi Fayed has also been killed. An unnamed French doctor has corroborated both fatalities."

I had grown unaccustomed to the English accent and it sounded foreign to me. Fiona gripped my hand and gaped at the television.

"Unconfirmed eyewitness reports say that paparazzi on motorcycles were pursuing Diana and Dodi's car at high speed immediately before the accident. We'll bring you more on this developing story as we receive it."

Fiona shook her head, and her eyes watered. "I can't believe this. She was my favourite royal. I knew those bastard photographers would be the death of her."

Sombre music played, and a head shot of a radiant Princess Diana wearing a blue dress and a diamond necklace filled the screen with hastily superimposed text:

> Diana, Princess of Wales
> 1st July 1961—31st August 1997

Fiona sobbed. "I never saw her. And now I never will."

Frank pressed his lips together and turned to me. "You'd better ring your father."

I glanced at the clock. "It's not yet six in the morning in England."

"You should call him anyway. He'll want to hear this news."

Fiona sat down heavily on the couch with her hands on her cheeks.

I lifted the receiver and dialled. "Dad, it's Simon. Sorry to wake you, but you need to turn on your television."

"Simon, is everything all right? Why are you ringing in the middle of the night?"

"Turn on the news."

"I'll switch on my bedside radio. Hang on."

Bedclothes rustled, followed by a loud click and the deep, slow voice of Radio 4.

"..flowers are already arriving at the palace. Mourners are standing at the gates in silence, holding hands in shock and grief."

"Who's died?" asked Dad. "Is it the Queen Mother? She would've been nearly ninety."

"It's not the Queen Mother. It's Princess Diana. She's been killed in a car crash."

"What? Goodness. I'll go downstairs and turn on the television. I'll call you later."

My father never ended phone conversations so abruptly.

I returned to the living room where Fiona gaped at the newscaster repeating the same announcement. She melted into my arms.

≈ ≈ ≈

Fiona stared out of the kitchen window a few days later. "I still can't believe it. I always wanted to see Princess Diana, and now I won't be able to. I so wish I'd glimpsed her when we lived in London."

"When's the funeral?" I asked. "We must watch it."

"They haven't announced a date. This caught them on the hop."

She clonked her breakfast plate in the sink, wiped her eyes and grabbed her car keys. "Anyway, how's calving going? D'you enjoy it as much as milking the cows?"

"Good. I'm loving it. They're so cute. I fed nine yesterday, but there'll be loads coming now; it's going to be a busy few weeks."

Fiona smiled at my enthusiasm. "Have you become a dad yet?"

"No, but I studied how Phillip assisted with a birth. I think I know what to do."

Jazz barked outside as the four-wheel bike's engine started. I shovelled in Nutri-grain as fast as I could. "Have a great day at work. I have to find today's babies with your mum."

I left my bowl on the kitchen bench, tugged on my boots and wet weather gear and ran outside.

The rain pinged against my face as we headed out along the gravel track towards the herd, and I stared at the ground to stay dry. Jazz rode behind me and shook himself regularly, his tongue lolling from the side of his mouth. Linda drove into the field, and we discovered miniature cows dotted around the paddock standing adjacent to full-size versions.

"This one's dead," said Linda. "Grab the other one. I'll turn the bike around."

I glanced at the deceased calf but didn't have time to feel sad as Linda immediately circled the bike, jumped off and opened the trailer's cage. I stretched my arms under a baby and lifted it up. Linda held the cage closed as the infant bleated non-stop, and its mother nuzzled it through the side, mooing loudly.

"Next one," said Linda.

I picked up another. She opened the gate quickly, and I shoved it in the cage before the first calf realised it had an escape route. Two mothers followed the trailer as we drove further into the field. The bleating noise level increased.

Linda stopped. "Quick, grab these two."

"Why do some calves die?" I lifted a third baby and made a mental note to purchase some earplugs.

"Some calves are born too early, some mothers give birth in the drains or the mud, some never take their first breath," she shouted. "Quite normal, unfortunately. It doesn't matter if they're boys."

I wasn't sure what this remark meant. Was she being sexist?

I picked up fourth and fifth calves and shoved them in the trailer while Linda prevented the others from absconding. We drove towards a further group at the back of the field.

"Grab these, and we'll come back for the rest. The trailer holds eight."

She held the gate, and I crammed in three more pony-sized babies. I watched Linda fight with an All Black rugby scrum of calves who wouldn't allow her to close the trailer. Eight Friesian mothers pursued us across the field, and I clamped my hands over my ears and wished the noise of bleating calves and mooing cows would go away.

Linda backed the trailer into the calving shed as I grabbed churns of milk and poured them into big, blue hanging buckets with a hedgehog of teats poking out from their sides. The calves clambered over each other to drink and each made a sucking noise like a Hoover that's been accidentally stuck into a puddle. I wondered whether they cared about being attached to a plastic, surrogate mother.

"Simon, pull the big one off. She's finished, and she's stealing the others' food."

I tugged the calf's head. She was determined to drink everybody's milk, and a mere lad from London wasn't going to stop her.

The bucket emptied, and the calves took a breather.

"Right," said Linda. "It's time to separate the boys."

She grabbed a baby and looked underneath it. "This one's male. Shove it in the trailer."

"Where are we taking them?"

"I'll show you in a minute. Grab this one, too."

I lifted the boy calves into the trailer.

"Damn," said Linda. "Another boy." She pushed the calf towards me.

The sorting process produced five male calves, standing in the trailer and looking slightly bewildered.

"Now what?" I said.

"Now we take the trailer and leave it at the farm entrance."

I scratched my head. "What, out on the road?"

"Yep." She jumped on the bike and started the engine. "Are you coming?"

I closed the shed gate to ensure none of the valuable female calves bolted, and we motored slowly along the farm's driveway. The boy calves braced themselves against the movement of the trailer and looked around at this new, exciting three-day-old world. The bike arrived at the end of the driveway. Linda unhitched the trailer, yanked the day's *West Coast Times* out of the mailbox, and we drove back to the farmhouse. I glanced back at the trailer with the calves in it and frowned.

"What happens to them? Does another farmer collect them and grow them into bulls?"

"No," said Linda. "The bobby calf man removes them."

I scratched my head. "Bobby calf man?"

I had an image of a creepy, long-haired, black-hatted character resembling the child catcher in *Chitty Chitty Bang Bang*.

Linda stopped outside the farmhouse and stepped off the bike. She looked at me, her mouth in a straight line. "At this time of year, there are too many male calves. It's not economic to feed them and keep them all. We'll grow some for breeding or beef but the rest go to the bobby calf man."

I rubbed the back of my neck. "This bobby calf man. What does he do with the boy calves?"

Linda frowned. "Have you ever seen veal on a restaurant menu?"

"I have. I thought it meant a different cut of beef."

"If you venture up to the road this afternoon, could you fetch the trailer? It'll be empty by then."

My mouth turned down, and I spun on my heels to stare at the end of the driveway where the little black animals stood in the red trailer. I imagined how disorientated and terrified they'd be, born into a new world a couple of days ago, separated from their parents, shoved in a trailer and abandoned at the side of the road, waiting for the spooky bobby calf man to put an end to their short lives. I wondered if their mothers warned them about the bobby calf man to persuade them to behave, as human parents threatened their offspring with the bogeyman.

Linda observed my expression. "I know it's not nice, but it's the reality of country living."

My eyes watered and I balled my fists. "I'll tell you something. I am never, ever eating veal."

≈ ≈ ≈

Linda dumped the paper on the table in front of Frank.

I sat in silence with my elbows on the table and my head in my hands.

"D'you want a sandwich?" asked Linda, interrupting my study of the tablecloth.

I sighed. "Could I have egg salad, please? I'm not sure I can eat meat today."

Frank looked up. "Would you be all right by yourself for a couple of hours? Linda and I have to drive to town this afternoon for an appointment."

"Where's Phillip?"

"He's out with his family. I'm not sure when they're coming back; sometime later."

I recalled the panic I'd had last time I'd been left alone on the farm, when everyone disappeared and I tried to milk the cows by myself.

"We won't be far away," said Frank. "We'll return before dinner. You'll be fine."

≈ ≈ ≈

Frank's car created a plume of dust as they departed. I stared after it and noticed the red trailer no longer contained little black-and-white animals.

"Here, Jazz."

The dog jumped on the four-wheel bike behind me. We motored out to the road, hooked up the empty trailer and returned to the farmhouse. It was as if the boy calves had never existed.

Now what needs doing? I'm in charge. This is my farm. I'm responsible for everything.

The girl calves slept in their shed. One looked up at me briefly.

All well here. They're not due for their milk until later.

I strolled around the yard, inspected the tractors, filled the bike with petrol, checked the gates and made sure I'd cleaned the calf feeders for the babies' evening meal. The milking machines dangled from their hooks ready for the afternoon's activities. I leant on the gate and met eyes with Shazam, the huge Friesian breeding bull. He snorted at me and rubbed his flank against a fencepost.

It's all right for you. Your job's done for this year.

The overcast, dark-grey sky threatened torrential rain. I hopped on the bike with Jazz, and we puttered along the track towards the herd who stood with their heads bent to the verdant meadow.

Three new calves sucked on their mothers' udders, and one black-and-white cow lay alone on the opposite side of the field. I pressed my finger to my lips.

Something's not right with her. Why is she lying there?

I climbed over the gate to investigate.

She looked up at me.

I looked back at her.

Two little hooves poked from her rear end.

19. GIVE ME THE NIGHT

The protruding feet didn't seem to bother the cow, and she turned around to inspect the forthcoming arrival.

Is she struggling to pass the calf?

I rolled up my sleeves and puffed out my chest.

This is it. Time for me to become a dad.

I vaulted the gate and reached into the bike's bucket.

Surgical equipment needed.

Metal rods: check.

Twine: check.

Legs sticking out: check.

The cow hadn't moved, but her additional legs had become longer. I strode towards her and paused.

Recap: how did Phillip do this?

Cross the poles.

Tie the twine to the legs.

Tug gently, but firmly.

I knotted the twine around the protruding legs and pulled it experimentally. The cow turned her head and surveyed me with a mildly bemused expression. I remembered how Phillip had to lean back a long way to pull his calf out, but this cow lay down on her side, and I couldn't figure out how to do the leaning bit. I knelt behind her and heaved. The legs extended slightly towards me.

Yes. This is going to work. I'm going to become a dad.

I angled back on my knees, put out my hand to steady myself and immediately experienced the warm squishiness of a freshly laid cow pat. Lush, green grass made suitable toilet paper, and I wiped my fingers. I tugged the twine again. With a slurping sound like vacuuming jelly, a black-and-white body slid out. The cow hoisted herself to her feet and tended to her newborn while the calf shook its head.

"Yes!" I shouted at the sky. "I'm a dad."

A tingling swept up the back of my neck as I realised I had an audience.

Phillip dangled his arms over the gate and grinned. "Simon, what are you doing?"

"I'm helping this cow give birth. I saw her lying down with two little hooves sticking out, so I remembered how you used the metal poles and the twine and I pulled the calf from her."

Phillip laughed. "She would've been fine by herself; she hadn't started pushing this morning."

I clasped my hands and looked at my feet. "I just wanted to become a dad like Frank said."

"Well done. Grab the trailer and we'll fetch these three new ones."

≈ ≈ ≈

"Hello?"

"Is that London Musician Simon Michael Prior?"

"It is. How can I help?"

"My name's Vicky. I'm on the committee of an event in Westport called Friday Frenzy. We're closing the main road for a street carnival to kick-start business after the winter. I run a jewellers, and I wondered if you could play some music outside my shop during the afternoon to keep the crowds entertained?"

Wow. A big, outdoor, live event. This is my dream.

"I'd love to. What date is the carnival?"

"Friday the 24th of October. Could you set up before noon and play from two until four p.m? It'd be fantastic to have you there."

I bounced from my left foot to my right foot. "That sounds great. Thank you for asking me."

≈ ≈ ≈

The gravel-scrunch of Fiona's car interrupted my humming as I laid out cutlery for dinner. I flung the door open, picked her up and spun her around so fast she dropped her handbag.

"What's all this about?" she asked. "Why are you so pleased with yourself?"

I retrieved her bag, lifted my heels and grinned. "The organisers of a big carnival in Westport phoned. They've booked me to play in the main street as part of the event entertainment."

"You're getting your name out there. How did they find out about you?"

I shrugged. "I'm not sure. Maybe someone saw me perform at a pub, or they heard an advert on Scenicland FM."

"How much are they paying?"

"$150 to play from two until four p.m."

"That's not much for driving to Westport; it's over two hours away. You won't have any money left after you've paid for petrol and lunch."

We entered the hut, and Fiona pulled her shoes off. "Why don't you call pubs along the carnival route, to see if they'll hire you for the Friday and Saturday nights? If you had three bookings for the weekend it'd be worth your while."

I poured her the end of a bottle of chardonnay. "Good idea. I'll look in the phone book tomorrow."

≈ ≈ ≈

"Hello? The Star Tavern? I'm a musician from Hokitika playing at Friday Frenzy carnival on the 24th of October. You haven't heard of it? Never mind, would you like to hire a band for either evening that weekend? You don't book bands. Okay, thanks, bye."

"McManus Hotel? I'm a musician based in Hokitika appearing at Friday Frenzy on the 24th. It's a street carnival to drum up business after winter; I thought you would've seen something about it. Anyway, I wondered if you wanted to book a band for the weekend? You've already arranged one. Okay, no problem."

"Hi, the Westport Pub? I'll be playing music at the Friday Frenzy next month. Ah, good, you've seen posters about it. Do you need a band afterwards? You'll come and see me on the street, and if I'm any good you'll pay me to perform at the pub in the evening. Um, okay."

I sighed and replaced the receiver. This was like selling Everest double-glazing.

Linda dumped a pile of clean laundry on the sofa. "Are you having a ring around?"

"Yep. A big carnival in Westport's engaged me to play, and I'm trying to arrange more bookings while I'm there."

"Any luck?"

"One pub might employ me for the Friday night, but he wants to hear me at the event before he confirms."

"Keep trying. Call the little towns outside Westport too."

I puffed out my cheeks, exhaled, and flipped to the next page in the phone book. "Good afternoon. Is that the Minersville Tavern?"

"Yep."

A deep voice. I imagined the person at the other end of the phone to resemble a professional rugby coach.

"My name's Simon Michael Prior. I'm a musician based in Hokitika, and I'll be playing at the Friday Frenzy in Westport. Have you heard about it?"

"Nope."

"It's a big outdoor party, planned for the 24th of October. They'll be closing off Palmerston Street to traffic, and there'll be market stalls, and a parade, and I'm playing outside the Heritage Jeweller's shop. I thought you might need a band on Saturday night. I can offer you a special rate of three hundred dollars as I'll be in Westport anyway."

"Right-oh."

I heard the flick of turning calendar pages.

"Yep."

"Yes, you need a band on Saturday evening?"

"Yep."

"Wonderful. Saturday it is."

I wrote in my diary. "What's your name, please?"

"Tane."

"Thanks, Tane. Oh, and what time d'you want me to start?"
"Seven o'clock. Bowls Club dinner."
"Ah, I understand. Thanks, I'll see you then."

The effort of pushing out a sentence longer than one word had clearly exhausted Tane, as he replaced the handset without saying goodbye. I ran outside and called to Fiona.

"I've arranged another booking. The Minersville Tavern."

"Minersville? D'you mean the little town north of Westport? I've seen the name on a map, but I've never been there."

≈ ≈ ≈

A man balancing on the top rung of a Himalaya-sized stepladder blocked Westport's main thoroughfare. Another worker who wore an orange, reflective vest braced the ladder's bottom with his feet.

He addressed me as I wound down my driver's window. "Won't be a minute, just fixing the bunting."

His colleague descended to the stepladder's base camp, and I cruised into Palmerston Street. Two rows of trestle tables shrouded in white paper bordered the roadway, and a selection of middle-aged ladies and men frantically arranged heavy objects to prevent the breeze from blowing everything into the next suburb. I switched on my hazard warning lights and crept forward until I discovered the green shop front of Heritage Jewellers, where I parked under a speaker mounted on a lamp post.

"You're listening to Fifeshire FM," said an enthusiastic lady announcer's voice. "We're so excited, because this afternoon, it's Friday Frenzy, a carnival right up and down Palmerston Street. So, if you're sitting at home doing nothing, come on down to Friday Frenzy for a fantastic afternoon of entertainment, stalls and the grand parade. That's Friday Frenzy, folks, this afternoon from two p.m."

The announcer's voice segued into Abba's 'Dancing Queen'.

A dark-haired girl of about fifteen responded to the shop bell's tinkle by briefly looking up from her study of *Cleo* magazine.

"Hi," I said. "Is Vicky here?" I pointed behind me with my thumb. "I'm the musician she hired to play outside."

"She's helping out in the street somewhere. She said you should set your gear up in front of the shop and she'll return soon."

The teenager twirled her curly hair around her finger and recommenced her research into *Buffy the Vampire Slayer*.

I smiled at her. "Okay, no problem. Thank you."

I tugged my amplifier and speakers from my car, placed them on the pavement and pointed them towards the road.

A lady assembling a stall on the opposite side of the street crossed over. "Hello. Are you playing music today?" She leant on my speaker with one plump hand.

"Yep. I'm London Musician Simon Michael Prior."

"Wow. Have you come from England?" She called to her colleagues. "Maylene, Brenda, quick, get over here. There's a guitar chap who's come all the way from London to play at our carnival."

"I'm from England originally," I said, "but I didn't travel from London just to perform at the Westport Friday Frenzy."

I clenched my teeth and squeezed my eyes closed as I realised how my words had come out wrong.

"You didn't?"

"Erm, no. I live in Hokitika now."

The woman turned to her friends. "Nothing to see here, ladies. This musician said he came from London, but he doesn't; he's from Hokitika."

They returned to their stall, and I resigned myself to the loss of three supporters before I'd begun.

My equipment sprawled over the pavement.

Power. Where would I find power?

The teenager folded her *Cleo* and examined the centrefold.

"D'you know where I'd find the nearest power point?" I asked. I banged the sides of my closed fists together in front of me to demonstrate the motion of connecting a plug to a socket.

She crouched and searched near her feet. "There's one here behind the counter."

"Okay. D'you own an extension lead?"

"Um, I don't know. Can you wait until Vicky returns?"

"Sure. I'll move my car and pop back soon."

I cruised slowly towards the Tango-vested stepladder man, who unclipped a rope to allow me through. I leant out of the driver's window. "Where's the best place to park for the day?"

He placed a hand on my car roof and pointed to a side street. "Pop it down there behind the Fifeshire FM building."

I positioned the car between two others, stepped out and gazed at the radio station's glass-fronted reception area.

This must be the local equivalent of Scenicland FM. Maybe they could mention my performance in their broadcast?

The door swung open as a man exited, and the same announcer's voice I'd heard in the street radiated from ceiling speakers.

"It's Friday Frenzy, folks, and it's one hour until we get going. The sun's shining, the entertainment's ready and the stalls are filled with exciting goods to buy, so come on down to Palmerston Street for the biggest afternoon of the year."

The annoyingly popular 'Barbie Girl' song followed as I set my jaw and approached the receptionist, who smiled at me from behind her rectangular-framed Dolce and Gabbana spectacles.

"Can I help you?"

"Hi. My name's Simon Michael Prior. I'm a musician playing in Palmerston Street as part of Friday Frenzy."

"Oh, yes. You're here for the live interview, right?"

I clenched my teeth and rubbed the back of my neck.

Has she mistaken me for someone else?

"Um, sure."

She picked up a ball-point pen in her immaculately-fingernailed hands and wrote my name on a pad.

"Great, I'll tell Karen."

"Karen?"

"Karen Fox. The lunchtime presenter."

This was all happening rather suddenly.

The receptionist ushered me into a small, windowless room. Through a glass door, I observed a young lady with wavy blonde hair gesticulate and speak into a vertical, flat microphone. A red light above the door glowed 'on air'. She removed her headphones, flicked a switch and opened the door.

The red light extinguished, and an enthusiastic male voice declared anyone who test drove a car at Westport Toyota would be entered into a draw to win a Hilux pickup truck.

"Karen?" said the receptionist. "This is Simon Michael Prior, the Friday Frenzy musician; he's arrived for his live interview."

Beads of sweat crystallised on my forehead, and I smiled thinly.

"Fantastic," said Karen. "I'll announce you after these adverts. Have you brought your press briefing?"

20. RADIO GA GA

Press briefing? What's that?

I took a deep breath and blinked. I might never receive this much exposure again in my career. "Sorry, Karen, I didn't realise I needed one today."

Karen rolled her eyes at the receptionist. I wondered if her broadcasting career aspirations included employment at a regional radio station, filling the gaps between Toyota adverts with interviews of pub musicians.

"Never mind," she said. "Come on in."

She led me through the glass door. The smell of coffee accompanied a voice promoting twenty per cent off rump steak at Supervalue. I cleared my throat multiple times and wiggled my arms. She draped headphones around her neck and poised before her microphone.

"Okay, I'll ask you a few questions. Respond as if you're chatting with a friend. Relax and enjoy the conversation."

"Um, sure."

"Oh, and Simon, for goodness' sake, give me meaningful answers. If you respond with 'yes', I'll kill you."

She beamed and reminded me of a praying mantis preparing to consume its husband.

I smiled back like the dutiful male insect. "Sure, Karen. No problem."

"Great. We'll be on after this next ad."

"…spend over twenty dollars and enter the draw for a $500 House of Travel gift voucher. Fly into Friday Frenzy and you could jet out to Surfers Paradise tomorrow."

Karen clamped on the headphones, shook her hair and flicked a switch. Her expression transformed into a wide, bogus grin. "Fifeshire FM, it's twenty-five past one and it's a huge day today; it's Friday Frenzy, right up and down Palmerston Street, celebrating the fact summer is on its way, and in the studio we have one of the entertainment features, a very good afternoon to Simon Michael Prior; how are you?"

I licked my tongue around the inside of my mouth.

Shit, shit, shit. Calm down, Simon. Relax. Answer as if you're chatting with a friend.

"Hello, Karen. It's wonderful to be in Westport; it's a beautiful sunny day by the looks of it, a few clouds, but it should be excellent for a great afternoon."

Gaah. Where did that come from? She didn't ask you to present the weather.

"It certainly will be. Now, give us some background of when and where you started your musical career."

"I started performing in England some fourteen years ago with a school band I formed, mainly playing Deep Purple and Status Quo numbers. I've lived in New Zealand since Christmas of last year and I've been playing music on the West Coast since March."

Phew. Good summary; I'm off to a reasonable start. Shit, this is hard. Calm down, calm down.

My tongue sucked all the remaining moisture out of my cheek.

"So, how are you enjoying the West Coast?"

Oh, no, now she wants a travel review.

"I think the West Coast's a great place; it's brilliant to wake up in the morning and look at snow-capped mountains and see the crashing seas; I'm enjoying myself here."

"And of course, no underground tunnels to cruise to work in?"

Is she referring to Princess Diana, or am I supposed to report on the road conditions?

"Absolutely not; no traffic at all."

"Now, d'you have a specific style, or is it mapped around another musician?"

Help. What do I say? Think, Simon, think.

"I've noticed on the West Coast, people enjoy country and western music and also the good old '60s rock n' roll, so since I've been here I've included more in my repertoire."

Karen reset her praying mantis expression.

"We have, of course, 1997 hits; what's your record of the decade?"

Record of the decade? Quick, Simon. What was the tune playing when you entered?

"It has to be 'Barbie Girl'; I adore that song; a lot of people criticise it but it's so catchy; you hear people sing it in the street."

Karen laughed into her microphone and sang the chorus. "Classic. You won't be wearing your *Barbie* costume this afternoon?"

"I will not be, no."

"You'll be playing from two until four p.m. outside Heritage Jewellers. What can we expect?"

"Everything from the '60s to the '90s, a bit of country, a bit of rock, Oasis, Red Hot Chili Peppers, anything popular."

"Sounds awesome. Simon Michael Prior, thanks for talking to us; we look forward to hearing you this afternoon."

"Thank you, Karen."

She flicked a switch and removed her headphones, as Keith Richards played the first chords of 'Start Me Up'.

"Thanks, Simon," she said. "I don't remember an interview going so smoothly. You obviously do these frequently."

She shook my hand, and I observed my fingers tremble.

"No problem, Karen. Thank you for the airtime."

≈ ≈ ≈

I skipped out of the studio and punched the air.

Yes! I survived live radio. I'm famous.

I paused and waited to hear if the ceiling speakers announced anything else about me. Keith Richards faded into Karen's voice, and I pictured her forcing the fake grin.

"Fifeshire FM, it's Friday Frenzy, starting at two p.m. all along Palmerston Street. The time's 1.30 so we'll head to the newsdesk for an update."

Maybe the newscaster will mention my forthcoming performance too?

"Good afternoon. Breaking news from Fifeshire FM; Friday Frenzy begins in half an hour. If you're planning on coming down to Palmerston Street, bring a shopping bag, your dancing shoes and plenty of spending money. Now, to overseas developments. The US has sent aircraft carrier *Nimitz* to the Persian Gulf.."

My fifteen seconds of fame evaporated as significantly less-important world news disseminated over the airwaves. I marched out of the glass doors and gazed along the street.

Where is everyone?

A lady dusted necklaces and rings in glass cabinets and minutely adjusted cardboard advertising. I coughed behind her.

"Hello, would you be Vicky?"

She turned around.

"I'm Simon Michael Prior."

"Hi, Simon, I heard you on the radio. I didn't realise they'd interview you today."

I twisted my head to one side and smiled. "I didn't realise they'd interview me either, but here we are."

She flapped out her cloth and a James Herbert fog of dust formed in front of her.

"Thanks for the mention of the jewellers. The promotion should encourage people to come."

"I hope so," I said. "The street seems a bit..quiet?"

"I'm sure you'll attract the crowds once you start playing. The committee's so pleased we persuaded you to appear. Famous international talent will put our town on the map."

Famous? International talent? Oh dear.

An antique clock in her window dinged.

"It's two o'clock," I said. "I'd better kick off."

"Of course. See you afterwards."

A black power cable draped over my amplifier, so I connected it, checked for the comforting *click* of my speakers and tapped the microphone twice to hear the familiar *doomp-doomp*. I slung my guitar around my neck, played a test chord, cleared my throat and glanced left and right.

A stallholder ate a sandwich and studied me in anticipation.

A dog performed yoga on the white line in the middle of the street and licked its bum.

Two boys executed wheelies along the road on their BMX bikes.

Time for my first big outdoor performance.

"Good afternoon, Westport. I'm London Musician Simon Michael Prior, and this is Friday Frenzy."

I began a medley of Beatles songs. A lady on a nearby stall clapped from her deckchair and sang along. After ten minutes of 'Twist and Shout', I extracted a piece of paper from my pocket and pretended to read it.

"And now, a special announcement from the vendors opposite. Could somebody please buy something? Anything?"

The stallholders laughed.

The breeze flapped the paper coverings.

The dog lifted its leg and peed liberally against a table.

≈ ≈ ≈

I finished at four p.m. with 'Crazy Little Thing Called Love'. The foot traffic hadn't increased, and Friday Frenzy had become Friday Frustration.

A small, thin man approached me. "Would you be Simon?"

"I am."

He dragged on a cigarette, flicked the butt onto the pavement and rotated his heel on it. "I'm from the Westport Pub. You rang me about playing at my venue."

I held out my hand. "Yes, what time do you need me to start?"

"Look, son, you're pretty good, but I can't afford a wash-out. There's no-one here. This Friday street carnival thing's a complete waste of time. They would have been better off putting on a bloody circus or something. Sorry, I can't employ you tonight."

"Oh, okay. Maybe another time?"

"Maybe."

He lit another cigarette and trudged away. I packed up my equipment. The speakers outside Fifeshire FM played 'Roll with It' by Oasis, and a male afternoon presenter had replaced Karen the mantis.

I checked into Western Backpackers, lay down on a bed, hugged myself and stared at the ceiling. I now faced a solo evening, with nothing to do, in this small, empty town where I knew no-one, followed by a whole day to fill before my next performance in a smaller town even further away from home.

I'd never felt more alone.

≈ ≈ ≈

I awoke in the middle of a terrifying nightmare, where I performed 'The Gambler' on stage to a deserted hall, but in place of a guitar I held a bleating calf. Dennis Stark marched into the venue and jabbed his finger at me. "You're bloody useless, you pommy prick. You can't attract one person to your so-called concerts. That calf's got more talent than you. Piss off back to England where you belong."

Sun streamed through the window of the backpackers. A lagoon of sweat soaked the clammy sheet, and I sat up, rubbed my eyes and ruffled my hair. Dennis Stark evaporated in a puff of invective.

I turned back the covers, wrapped a towel around myself and headed for the showers.

≈ ≈ ≈

'Welcome to Minersville', announced a road sign at the entrance to the tiny settlement where Tane, the man of few words, had booked me to entertain his bowls club.

O little town of Minersville, how still I see thee lie.

The town enjoyed a setting at the foothills of the Southern Alps, sprayed by the crashing waves of the Tasman. I wound the car window down and inhaled the wonderful smells of salt air and humid vegetation.

Translucent double pub doors creaked as I pushed them, and I peeked in and wondered if a sudden earthquake had compelled all the staff and customers to run away. My shoes clumped towards the bar on the polished wooden floorboards, and I tried to walk less obviously. I leant over the counter, cleared my throat and looked left and right.

Nobody.

Stairs ran to a second floor, and I craned my neck to see up them.

No sign of life.

Is this the right date?

I stood and tapped my fingers on the bar.

Now what do I do?

An area at the other end of the room served as a stage, so I heaved my gear over and set up. I plucked a test chord and strummed 'Don't Dream It's Over'. The music sounded echoey in the empty room. As I played to myself, a brown-skinned, black-haired young lady appeared behind the bar, rubbed her eyes, yawned and smiled. I paused.

"Don't stop," she said. "I love Crowded House. That song reminds me of my mum."

"Oh, hi there. I'm Simon, the musician."

"I'm Pania. I recognise you from the poster you sent us to pin up. But I didn't know you were playing tonight. Tane didn't mention anything about music."

She glanced down and hid her dark-brown eyes behind her hair.

"Tane's the landlord, right?" I asked.

"Yep, but he's out at his brother's. I'll call him and double check."

She lifted a phone handset mounted to the wall, and I overheard one side of a conversation.

"He asked if you could start around seven o'clock, to keep the bowls club entertained."

"No problem. I'll take a stroll and return later."

One car overtook me as I ambled along the main road which bisected Minersville. I passed a few wooden houses in various states of disrepair, many of which wouldn't have endured a strong breeze. At the end of the street, I discovered a rugby pitch, then the town finished, and the straight, one-lane highway which strung these remote West Coast communities together stretched into the distance.

I hadn't found a bowls club and wondered if anyone would turn up at all.

≈ ≈ ≈

Two men in checked shirts sat on bar stools when I returned, and one table contained an older couple waiting for dinner.

At least someone's here.

I approached a tall, fat, brown-skinned man who leant over the counter and talked to the men on the stools. He raised his eyebrows at me.

"Hi, would you be Tane?" I asked. "I'm Simon, your musician for tonight."

He didn't respond to this, apart from adjusting his stance slightly.

I pointed at my poster. "Thanks for putting the advert up, but I noticed you didn't write the date on it. D'you think people will know I'm playing?"

One of the customers answered. "There are only two hundred people living in this town; we don't need a poster to know what's going on."

He shifted on his stool and slurped his beer.

The other man spoke. "You're lucky to earn a gig here. Tane doesn't normally book bands."

Tane lifted himself off his elbows and poured a beer. He didn't offer me one. "Start at seven," he said. "Quietly."

I couldn't understand why he wanted me there at all.

≈ ≈ ≈

By seven o'clock, several diners sat at tables. Pania ferried meals and cleared plates. Tane served drinks to men and women who wore white shirts and trousers.

They must be the bowls club.

I strummed quietly, as requested. 'Summertime', from *Porgy and Bess*. Elevator music, that would disturb no-one.

The diners continued eating.

Pania continued waitressing.

The bowls club members continued chatting.

Tane may as well have played a Richard Clayderman tape.

An hour into the evening, I stepped outside to escape the Benson and Hedges smog. When I returned, a group of young Māori men waited in front of my gear. Koru tattoos encircled their arms and spread onto their necks. They displayed piercings and wore black singlets.

One turned to me when I shouldered my guitar. "Are you gonna play anything good tonight?"

He grinned eye teeth which had been filed to points.

"Something lively?" said another.

"I can play more upbeat music, sure."

The first one held out his hand. "What's your name?"

"I'm Simon. I come from Hokitika. Well, London, originally."

"I'm Ari. Tane never puts bands on usually. We've come here to be entertained."

His black, plaited hair hung over one shoulder and his bare upper arm muscles bulged from his sleeveless top. The others nodded and laughed.

"D'you play any reggae?" asked Ari.

"Sure."

I racked my brains to think of any song I knew which they would categorise as reggae.

'Three Little Birds'. Bob Marley and the Wailers. Nothing more reggae than Bob.

I tried to avoid assuming a Jamaican Patois accent but I needn't have worried. The Māori boys provided all the singing required. I segued into 'Swing Low, Sweet Chariot'. Technically an African-American spiritual, but Eric Clapton had recorded it as a reggae number so I figured it counted. Ari and his friends loved it. They sang, drank and danced. One of them bought a tray of beers and placed one in front of me.

8.30.

The bowls crowd stood in an ensemble at the bar and conversed loudly to compete with the Māori male voice choir. The young lads sang, stomped their feet, cheered and clapped. They ordered round after round of drinks.

This is an amazing night for such a small town. It's like my guest artist appearance in Christchurch.

I sang the opening line to 'Living Next Door to Alice'.

The Māori joined in. They yelled the alternative refrain at the correct points complete with all the profanities. They bought yet more beer.

This is going well. Tane'll be so pleased he booked me.

During 'Living Next Door to Alice' the bowls club members finished their drinks and departed. I hoped they'd enjoyed the entertainment. I wound down at eleven p.m. with 'Big Yellow Taxi'. One of the Māori had passed out, and the others tried to help him to his feet.

Ari shook my hand. "Thanks, Simon. The best night we've had in years. I'm gonna ask Tane to book you again."

"No problem, Ari. I'm glad you had fun. Thanks for the beer."

I packed up and approached the bar. "Hi, Pania. Is Tane around?"

"He's upstairs, but he left your money."

Her expression didn't seem as friendly as it had been.

She must be tired after a big night.

She handed me a cheque. I confirmed the details and stuffed it in my pocket.

≈ ≈ ≈

Now I had a three-hour midnight drive home on the remote West Coast Road, so I shoved my loudest tape into the car music player, opened the driver's window and left Minersville in my rear-view mirror. My mind buzzed with the euphoria of success.

The singing.

The dancing.

The audience participation.

I balled one fist, shook my forearm and shouted, "Yes!" into the darkness.

The absence of stars outlined black jagged peaks to my left. Small farming settlements flashed past at 100 kilometres per hour.

Not a single person awake.

Not a single light.

Not a single car.

After 45 minutes, I slowed down to Westport's urban speed limit. The town had dismantled Friday Frenzy, and light shone from deserted shop fronts. Less than half a tank of fuel showed on my gauge, but the petrol pumps stood in darkness. My headlights lit up the sign announcing the end of Westport's speed restriction, and I sped into the black.

Black.
Night.
Tired.
Sleep.

I forced my eyelids open and leant out of the driver's window so cold air could hit my face. I still hadn't passed a single car, and I steered automatically.

My head jerked up, as the oncoming lights of a Westland Dairy milk tanker blinded me.

21. MONEY, MONEY, MONEY

My car bumped off the road and along the verge, as the tail lights of the tanker vanished behind me and its deep, prolonged air horn Dopplered into the night.

Shit, you went to sleep.

The rear wheels slipped as I regained the asphalt, accelerated slowly and stared at the white lines dividing the tarmac.

I opened alternate eyes.

I held one eye open with a finger and thumb.

I slapped my cheek.

Toto played 'Africa' as a brown sign came into view, pointing towards the sea. 'Scenic Viewpoint: 300 metres'. I steered into the gravel layby, turned the engine off, reclined the driver's seat and immediately slept to the sound of breakers crashing against the black cliffs below me.

≈ ≈ ≈

Sleep.

Sleep.

Ping.

Ping. Ping.

Cold drizzle spat through the car window and stung my face as I sat up and rubbed my eyes.

What time is it?

The clock's green light glowed from the dashboard.

3.45. If I continue now, I'll be home by five.

Toto sang further stanzas about Mount Kilimanjaro, as I spun the wheels and sped along the coast road to the farm.

≈ ≈ ≈

"D'you need anything in town, Linda?" I asked on Monday morning.

Linda opened the fridge and revealed shelves stuffed with Tupperware containers chronologically arranged from recent times back to the Cretaceous period.

"Could you pick up some juice? We're getting low. And cheese."

"Sure. See you at lunchtime."

I drove into town, parked outside the council offices and approached reception.

A middle-aged lady behind the desk negotiated into a phone. "Yes, madam. I know that drain cover's been broken for a while. We will fix it. I'm aware you've called us five times. No, I'm sorry, you still have to pay your rates in full. Yes, I appreciate how much they've gone up; I pay them as well. No, there's no need for you to come to the council offices in person; it won't make any difference. Yes, madam. No, madam. Thank you for calling."

She replaced the receiver. The phone immediately rang again.

I raised my hand and wiggled it. "Hi. Where would I find Mike Keenan, please?"

"Up the stairs, second office on the left."

She pointed with her left hand and lifted the phone receiver with her right. "Good morning, council offices. Missed rubbish collection? I'm sorry to hear that, sir. Just a tic, putting you through."

Her phone rang again as I climbed the stairs. I tapped on a door with a sign announcing: 'Mike Keenan—Events Manager'.

"Come in."

A man in his forties with brown hair sat behind a desk.

"Would you be Mike Keenan?"

The man stood, circumnavigated his desk and smiled with his entire face, as if my visit was the most important thing in his world.

He held out his hand and squeezed mine.

"I'm Mike." He gestured to a chair on my side of the desk. "Please, have a seat."

I sat, slightly nervous at his ebullient welcome. I suspected he'd mistaken me for someone else.

"Hi, Mike. I'm Simon Michael Prior, a musician from London living and working in Hokitika. You might have seen my posters in pubs around the town."

Mike reclined in his chair with his hands behind his head. He grinned again.

"I can't say I have, Simon, but go on."

"I go out with Frank Wall's daughter, Fiona. Frank suggested I come and chat with you. I understand you book bands for the Wild Foods Festival, and I hoped you'd consider me as one of the acts for next year."

He nodded and leant forwards. "I'm sure we could. What kind of music d'you play?"

"The '60s to the '90s; the usual classic hits. I've learnt some country and western, too."

"Sounds good. I'll find an application form."

He swivelled his chair to face a filing cabinet, opened the top drawer, riffled through papers and extracted a single white page headed 'Wild Foods Festival 1997: Entertainment Application Form'. He crossed out the '7' and wrote '8'.

"There we go. You're the first applicant. I'll have to print new ones for next year. Could you fill in the details?"

He passed me a ball-point pen, and I completed my name, address and phone number. I noted '1' in the box for the number of members in my band and wrote 'classic rock' as my music genre. I slid it back to him.

"Thanks. I'll be in touch a few weeks before the festival. But I'm sure we'll find you a spot."

"Great, thanks, Mike. I look forward to hearing from you."

I closed the door behind me, threw my head back and fist-pumped the air.

I'm a rock star. I'm headlining the Wild Foods Festival.

I skipped down the street, stopped at the Bank of New Zealand and swung open the glass entrance.

≈ ≈ ≈

"Good morning, Shirley."

"Hi, Simon. D'you have more music earnings to pay in? Where've you been playing this time?"

I tugged Tane's cheque from my pocket, slid it through the slit between us, and she plucked it off the counter.

"Oh, wow, Minersville. That's a fair distance up the Coast. I've never been there. Did you have a good night?"

"Fantastic, thanks. There's a lively, fun crowd there; I had them all singing along."

She laid the cheque in front of her keyboard and tapped details into her computer while I flicked through marketing information enticing me to take out a huge mortgage in the unlikely event I ever saved twenty per cent for a house deposit. Shirley peered at her screen.

I furrowed my brow and replaced the pamphlet in a cardboard display. "Is everything okay?"

"I think so; just a sec."

She poked 'delete' multiple times and entered the cheque details again, more slowly.

She pressed the return key and frowned.

I leant forwards to see her screen. "What's wrong?"

"This cheque won't enter. I'm not sure why. Hold on, let me fetch the manager. Sorry about this."

She knocked on the door of a rear office and returned accompanied by a short, fat man in a white shirt and a tie striped in the bank's corporate colours. He nodded at me and bent over Shirley's computer. She showed him the cheque and the details she'd entered.

He pointed at her screen. "See this symbol here? It means the cheque's been stopped. It's not valid and can't be cashed."

I stuck out my bottom lip and drew my head back.

"You'll need to speak to the account holder, Mr Prior," he said. "For some reason, they've stopped this payment."

I shook my head. "Stopped the payment?"

Shirley passed the cheque to me across the counter. "Sorry, there's nothing we can do with it."

≈ ≈ ≈

I leant on the kitchen table with my face in my hands. Linda plopped a plate of sandwiches in front of me.

Frank opened the kitchen door, hung up his green farm jacket and kicked off his Wellington boots. "What are you looking upset about, Simon?"

"I played at the Minersville Tavern on Saturday. The evening went well; I performed to a lively crowd; they sang along, bought loads of drinks, and enjoyed the music. The pub gave me a cheque, but when I tried to pay it in at the bank, Shirley said it'd been stopped, and she couldn't cash it."

Frank cupped his chin in his hand. "I wonder what's wrong? Have you asked the landlord?"

"Not yet."

"Give him a ring."

I referred to the phone book, picked up the handset and dialled.

"Yep?" said a man's voice.

"Is that the Minersville Tavern?"

"Yep."

"Is Tane there?"

"Yep."

Silence.

"Is that Tane?"

"Yep."

"It's Simon Michael Prior speaking, the musician you hired on Saturday."

"Yep."

"I, err, tried to cash the cheque you gave me, and they said it's been stopped; it's not valid."

"Yep."

"Why is it stopped, Tane? What's wrong?"

"You didn't do as I asked."

I rubbed my forehead. "You booked me to play music. I played music."

"I wanted you to play background music to entertain the bowls club. Not to shout and swear at my customers. Don't ask me for money again."

He hung up and left me staring at the receiver.

"Did you hear that, Frank? He won't pay me. What do I do?"

Frank's face formed a conspiratorial grin. "I'll tell you exactly what we're going to do. We'll go legal. We're going to sue."

"Sue the landlord, Frank? You mean, take him to court?"

"Yes," said Frank. "That's exactly what we'll do." He rubbed his hands together so hard I expected smoke to rise from them. "This is going to be fun."

"But we're talking about three hundred dollars. Is it worth it?"

"It's the principle, the principle. We can't allow him to get away with not paying you." He held up one finger and winked at me. "Plus, we're going to win."

"How d'you know?"

"I say we're in with a good chance. The local magistrate's an old horse racing friend of mine."

≈ ≈ ≈

Frank parked outside the Greymouth courthouse, and we approached a lady behind a desk. "Hello," I said. "Could I have the form you need to err.."

Frank completed my sentence. "We want to take legal action in a tribunal, please."

The lady studied him over her horn-rimmed glasses. "What is the value of the claim? Is it over or under five thousand dollars?"

"Under," I said. "Significantly under."

She stood, opened a filing cabinet behind her and drew out a two-page document. "Please fill in both pages and pay the fee of $36 to arrange a hearing." She pointed behind us. "There's a pen on the counter if you wish to complete it here."

I sat at the desk and filled in my name and address. Frank peered over my shoulder.

"What amount should I put as my claim?" I asked. "Three hundred dollars?"

"I reckon we should demand more."

Frank paced with his hands behind his back, his chest puffed out and his head up. "What about your petrol, your time and the fees for this application?" He faced a mirror behind us, held his jacket lapels and addressed his reflection.

"And the damage to your reputation. I mean, if people learn about this, you might lose bookings. It might threaten your chances of playing at the Wild Foods Festival. It's bordering on slander. I reckon you should demand thousands. Tens of thousands."

I ran my fingers along the small print. "Err, the notes say you're not allowed to apply for those sorts of costs at this level. Those are for more important cases in a higher court."

Frank pursed his lips. "Shall we go for a higher court?"

I rolled my eyes at him, wrote 'three hundred dollars', signed the form and handed it to the court clerk. She checked my work by marking primary school teacher-red ticks, stamped the form and wrote me a receipt.

"You'll receive a letter when the date's set for the tribunal, Mr Prior. It should be a couple of weeks. You're permitted to bring one supporter with you, such as a witness or personal referee."

I climbed into the passenger seat of Frank's car, and we drove away.

He tapped his fingers on the steering wheel and shook his head. "I still think we should've asked for more money."

≈ ≈ ≈

Frank knocked on the hut window as I practised new material the following week. "Phone, Simon."

I followed him into the kitchen, and he passed me the handset. "It's Tom Newell."

I took the receiver and covered the mouthpiece. "Who's Tom Newell?"

"He was the Mayor of Haast last time I heard. Pretty wealthy chap by reputation. I wonder what he wants with you?"

"Hello?"

"G'day, Simon. Tom Newell calling. How are you today?"

"Fine, thanks, Tom."

I glanced back at Frank and shrugged.

"I understand you play music," said Tom. "Would you be able to entertain the guests at my fiftieth birthday party on the thirteenth of December?"

"Yes, I'm not booked that evening. Whereabouts are you holding it?"

"At Okuru village hall. Down the road from my home."

"You live in Haast, don't you?"

"I do. Born and bred."

"I'd love to play for your party, but Haast's four hours' drive south. It's a long way to travel for one performance."

"Simon, I'll make it worth your while. Will $500 plus $150 for petrol be enough? And I'll book you a room at the pub for the night."

$650 plus accommodation.

I nodded and puffed out my cheeks. "I reckon so. Is there anything particular you want me to play?"

"There'll be people of all ages attending, so a mixture of old songs and more recent ones would suit the occasion. Oh, and d'you know 'Thank God I'm a Country Boy?' It's a favourite of mine."

"No problem. I'll make sure I learn it."

For $650, I'll master Rachmaninoff's Third Symphony.

≈ ≈ ≈

Linda entered the kitchen and dumped a stack of mail and newspapers next to a volcano of lunchtime toasted sandwiches. "There's a letter here for you, Simon," she said. "It looks official."

Frank glanced at the envelope. "It must be from the court. It'll be the date for your tribunal."

He rubbed his hands together and grinned. I flipped the letter over and back again. I read the tiny writing in the top left corner and ran my finger along the seal.

"Open it, then," said Frank. He smiled and nodded rapidly. "Don't keep us waiting."

I slit the envelope with a knife and pulled out two pages of photocopied form, populated in scribbly handwriting that seemed to have been written by an inebriated spider. I scanned from the top and stopped at the middle of the first paragraph.

My jaw fell open, and my hand covered my mouth.

Frank snare-drummed his fingers on the table. "Well? What's the date of the tribunal?"

I shook my head and stared at him. "It doesn't mention a date. The landlord's counter-sued me for two thousand dollars."

22. BRASS IN POCKET

"What d'you mean, counter-sued you?" asked Frank.

I handed him the letter, and he skimmed it.

"... loss of business... damage to reputation... costs for hiring a bus to transport twenty witnesses to court..." He paused and looked up. "I thought you couldn't ask for those?"

"I should never have brought this case," I said. "I'll cut my losses and drop the proceedings."

He removed his spectacles, leant on his elbows and looked at me. "Remember the first rule of litigation: if you're going to threaten action against someone, you have to be prepared to follow through."

He grinned. "Anyway, it's just become interesting."

He replaced his glasses and re-read the court letter.

I looked at him and bit my nails. "But I don't have two thousand dollars to pay the landlord if I lose. What am I going to do? I can't go ahead with this."

"Don't worry. As I said, we're going to win. I'll help you, and I'll be your supporter at the tribunal. Grab a pen, and we'll reject the counter-claim."

He swivelled the form towards me. "Tick this box here: 'I reject the counter-claim', and this one, where you say you wish to proceed with the tribunal."

My pen shook so violently I missed the tick-box and I had to mark it again.

Frank tapped the form. "Now sign here and date it here."

I drew a signature which meandered across the page like one of the more remote Amazon tributaries and wrote the date.

"Slip it in the envelope," said Frank, "and we'll return it to the court."

I glanced at him and bit my lip. "Are you one hundred per cent sure about this?"

He nodded. "I've never been more certain, Simon. Never been more certain."

≈ ≈ ≈

Frank and I sat in the corridor outside the courtroom. I wriggled in my seat and smoothed down my borrowed suit, as my mind cycled through multiple potential outcomes.

Maybe Tane won't find a bus for all these witnesses?
Maybe he won't turn up at all?
Maybe he'll arrive and immediately pay me?

Frank crossed his legs and rested his clasped hands in his lap. He turned and gave me a slight smile. The door creaked open, and Tane and Pania entered. I looked behind them to count their twenty witnesses, but they all seemed to have excused themselves for more important engagements. Tane and Pania sat on the opposite side of the corridor.

Three of us found the waiting room ceiling cornice design fascinating.

Frank ignored the architecture.

He studied our adversaries.

At two p.m. the courtroom door opened, and a small, balding man wearing a tweed jacket and dark trousers poked his head out. "Good afternoon. Are you all here for Prior versus Henare?"

"We are," said Frank. He stood and buttoned his suit jacket.

I gulped. Tane inclined his head.

"Would you all please enter the courtroom?" said the magistrate. He met eyes with Frank and gave a slight nod.

We filed in obediently and sat on opposite sides of a large, wooden table. The magistrate installed himself at the head, between us. Tane stared upwards. I formed my fingers into a steeple and attempted to interpret his body language.

The magistrate rested his hands on a buff-coloured folder. "Welcome. My name's Anthony Morton, and I'll officiate over proceedings today and help both sides reach an agreement. First, I'll note everyone's names and whether they appear for the plaintiff or the defendant."

He looked up to ensure we had his attention. I wondered how many of these cases he heard each week, if any.

"The plaintiff will then present their statement as to why they're bringing this action, why they feel their case is justified, and what result they hope to achieve from the tribunal. While the plaintiff is speaking, the defendant must remain silent. Are we all clear?"

We nodded to show our compliance. Pania studied her lap and fingered her necklace.

"Following the plaintiff's statement, the defendant may respond and state whether they concur with the plaintiff, or whether they rebut their allegation. During this time, the plaintiff must themselves remain silent."

We nodded again. Anthony continued.

"I observe both sides are accompanied by supporters. Once the plaintiff and defendant have completed their statements, I'll allow each supporter to add any additional relevant points."

The flicker of a grin crossed Frank's face. Pania chewed her fingers and glanced downward. I wasn't convinced she was a willing participant.

"Finally," said Anthony, "once everyone's had a chance to speak, I'll summarise both points of view, and I'll make a decision which will be binding on both parties."

He paused and tapped his papers vertically for effect. "Are we ready? First, who appears for the plaintiff?"

I raised my hand slowly, like a kindergarten child who needs the bathroom.

"I do."

He referred to the paper in front of him. "You would be Simon Michael Prior?"

"I am."

"And you are accompanied, it would seem, by Frank Wall, of Hokitika. How are you, Frank? I haven't seen you since the Greymouth races."

Frank nodded once. "I'm well, thank you, Anthony."

Tane shuffled in his seat.

"And appearing for the defence, you are?"

"Tane Rawiri Henare, landlord of the Minersville Tavern."

"Thank you, Mr Henare. And finally, the young lady."

Pania spoke almost inaudibly. "Pania Taurua, your honour. I work for Tane."

"Call me Anthony, or Mr Morton, Miss Taurua. We reserve 'your honour' for the crown court."

"Yes, your honour. I mean, Mr Morton."

Anthony made notes on his front sheet. He flipped it over to a new, blank piece of paper and turned to me. "Mr Prior, please state your case."

Frank glanced at me and nodded.

I cleared my throat and leant forwards on my elbows. "I'm a musician, playing at pubs, clubs and parties up and down the West Coast. You may have seen posters advertising my performances."

"I haven't,' said Anthony, "but go on."

"Tane employed me to play music for four hours at the Minersville Tavern, from seven until eleven p.m. on Saturday the 25th of October. We agreed on a fee of three hundred dollars. I arrived early, set up my gear, checked in with Pania and departed for a stroll around the district. I returned shortly before seven and observed the pub contained a few diners and drinkers. Once seven o'clock came, I commenced at the beginning of my set where I play quieter music as people finish dining, before continuing with more energetic songs later in the evening. At around 8.30, a group of young people arrived. They bought a round of drinks and requested I perform some reggae."

"I wouldn't have called that noise reggae," interrupted Tane.

Anthony held his hand up. "Ah-ah-ah, Mr Henare. You'll have your chance to speak. Please permit the plaintiff to finish."

I huffed and rolled my eyes at Tane, an expression completely lost on Anthony, who made notes on his pad. "Anyway," I said, "the young people cheered and clapped and bought round after round of drinks, so I continued playing the music they requested. I figured Tane would be pleased they were enjoying themselves and spending money at the pub. At the end of the evening, I packed up, and Pania handed me a cheque signed by Tane. However.."

I paused for effect and glanced around my audience.

"..when I visited the bank the following Monday and tried to cash the cheque, the teller told me Tane had stopped it, and they couldn't give me my earnings. I rang Tane, who said he wasn't happy with my performance and he wouldn't be paying me."

"I see," said Anthony. He wrote silently, then looked up at me.

"Mr Prior, were you surprised Mr Henare had stopped the cheque?"

"Of course. The tavern had enjoyed a busy night, and he must've sold a lot of drinks. I imagined my performance would've delighted him."

Anthony inspected another piece of paper. "Were you also surprised to receive a counter-claim from Mr Henare for two thousand dollars?"

The first inkling I might win this case entered my mind. "Definitely. I saw no justification for the counter-claim. He booked me to play music, and I played music. I believed I'd kept my side of the agreement, and he should pay me in full."

"Is there anything else you wish to add, Mr Prior?"

"That's all, I think."

I leant back in my chair and put my hands behind my head.

That went surprisingly well. I can't see how Tane can defend his refusal to pay me.

Anthony wrote more notes and turned to Tane. "Mr Henare, you now have the opportunity to reply."

"Well," said Tane, "everything Simon's said is correct.."

Anthony raised his eyebrows.

Frank raised his eyebrows.

I raised my eyebrows.

If it's all correct, Tane, why didn't you pay me?

"..only he didn't mention the swearing."

I leant forwards and covered my mouth.

"The swearing, Mr Henare?" said Anthony.

"Yes. There's one song he plays; I think it's called 'Living Next Door to Alice', where he swears loudly throughout the whole song. The bowls club, who'd spent a significant amount of money on food and wine, turned around and walked out. The president said he thought I possessed better judgement than to book such a crude act."

I flexed my fingers and shook my head rapidly. "It's not a crude act."

Anthony held up his palm. "Hang on, Mr Prior. Mr Henare's allowed to speak without interruption."

"That's why I'm not paying him," said Tane. He stabbed the table with his forefinger. "I can't risk losing the bowls club's business, and I've told the president I haven't paid Simon and he won't be coming back to play his so-called music again."

Tane sat back in his chair. I puffed out my cheeks and gazed into my lap.

Anthony wrote several notes. "Now the plaintiff and the defendant have spoken, may I invite their supporters to add any relevant comments? Frank, I presume you weren't a witness to this event."

"I wasn't, Anthony, but may I state Simon's been living on my farm for the last few months, and you'd never find a harder worker who's more willing to help. Simon's learnt to milk the cows, bale the silage, drive the tractors, he's even feeding the calves. I don't think you could meet a more upstanding young man."

I shuffled in my seat.

"Thank you, Frank," said Anthony. "Miss Taurua, do you have anything you wish to say?"

Pania chewed the inside of her cheek and glanced sideways at Tane, who stared into his lap and didn't notice.

She spoke in a quiet voice. "I was there. It wasn't Simon who swore."

Tane's head jerked up and to the side. His eyebrows drew together and his body stiffened.

"Go on," said Anthony.

"The crowd of young people who entered the pub; I know them; one's my cousin. As Tane said, there's this song, 'Living Next Door to Alice'. They shouted a chorus to it. Simon sang the proper chorus, then they added their own part with the swear words."

I sat up and opened my eyes wide.

Anthony turned to Tane. "Is this what happened?"

"Well, yes," said Tane, "but Simon incited them; he encouraged them. There wouldn't have been all the swearing if he hadn't played that song. They're a rough crowd. I don't like them in the pub."

"Miss Taurua," said Anthony, "what swear words did they use?"

Her cheeks flushed.

Anthony passed her a piece of paper and a pen. "You can write them down if you don't feel comfortable saying them."

Pania wrote. I stretched my neck to see her handwriting without being obvious. Anthony took the paper and looked at it. His eyebrows raised, and he wrote more notes on his pad, produced a pocket calculator and pushed its buttons, then flipped back to the start and re-read his entire summation.

I tapped my foot and twiddled my thumbs. Tane formed a straight line with his mouth and watched the magistrate.

The outcome of a John Grisham murder trial wouldn't have been any less anticipated.

Anthony laid down his pen and cleared his throat dramatically.

"I have come to a decision," he announced.

Tane and I both leant forwards.

"I find Simon Michael Prior to be one-eighth at fault, for inciting these young pubgoers to shout obscenities and upset other customers of the Minersville Tavern. I find Tane Rawiri Henare seven-eighths at fault, for failing to keep to the original contract and failing to curtail the song in question by asking Simon to cease playing it. I therefore order Tane Rawiri Henare to pay Simon Michael Prior the sum of $262.50, being seven-eighths of the original sum agreed. Each of you will receive a copy of my findings. Should either side wish to appeal my decision, please ask for the relevant form at the front desk."

He smiled and nodded at us. "Thank you for attending today. The tribunal is over." He pushed himself up, tapped his papers and slipped his pen into an inside pocket.

Frank set his jaw and nodded while I pushed out my bottom lip and puffed a long breath. Tane grimaced and shook his head. Pania glanced at me, then looked away, as the four of us vacated the room in silence. I watched her step into Tane's car and wondered how their conversation would go during the drive back to Minersville.

Frank shook my hand on the pavement. "Fantastic result. I told you we'd win."

I grinned. "Thanks for your encouragement. When he started talking about the swearing, I thought I was done for."

"No chance. He didn't have a leg to stand on. Justice has been served."

"What now, Frank?"

"I think we'd better celebrate over a whisky, don't you?"

≈ ≈ ≈

The morning brought rain, which hammered on the tin roof and connected puddles to form a small reservoir in the driveway. I watched Fiona flick through the farm calendar while I spooned Nutri-grain. Various images of snow-capped mountains and ice-blue lakes accompanied scrawly announcements of vet's visits and doctor's appointments.

"What are you doing?" I asked.

She rested one finger flat on her lips. "What date did we leave Tonga and land in New Zealand?"

"Shortly before Christmas last year. Why?"

"Here we go again. This time it's your visa about to expire."

23. GO WEST

"I know my visa's about to expire, Fiona; it's valid for one year. But the lady at the airport said I could renew it."

"It won't be automatic. I'm sure you can't pop into the supermarket and buy one. We'll probably have to travel to Christchurch. At least, I hope it's Christchurch, and not Wellington. I don't want to fly to the North Island."

"Hmm. How do we discover what to do?"

"I've no idea. I've never had to apply for a New Zealand visa, have I? Let's find a phone number for the correct government department."

≈ ≈ ≈

The immigration lady peered at us over her Dame Edna Everage-glasses. She inspected Fiona, then me, then Fiona again. I listened to the tick of her wall clock and tapped my fingers together.

Her eyes finally settled somewhere above my fringe. "Thank you for coming to Christchurch today. My name's Ursula Bott, and I'll be assessing your application for a permanent visa."

She pushed grey, wavy hair away from her round shoulders, flicked through the pages of my completed form and gave us what I hoped passed for a smile. I imagined in a previous life she'd been employed as the headmistress of a particularly Draconian private school for girls.

"So," said Ursula, "you've been together as a couple for the past two years, first in England and now here?"

"Yes," I said. My voice had become tiny, as if she were telling me off for not cleaning behind my ears.

"And you've applied for a partner visa based on the longevity of this relationship?"

"Yes."

She glanced at my form again. "I require evidence you're a de facto married couple living together as if you were husband and wife, for a period in excess of one year. What have you brought today to demonstrate this?"

She sat back in her chair and folded her arms.

I unstuck the flap of an A4-sized, brown folder and extracted several sheets of paper. "Here are letters from Fiona's family, addressed to both of us at the flat where we lived in London."

Ursula scanned the letters briefly. "They don't have a date."

"Yes, they do. At the top."

"Anyone could have written that. D'you possess the original envelopes with the postmarks?"

"Sorry, I don't."

I tugged another item from the folder and slid it towards her. "Here's a photograph of me and Fiona taken on top of the Eiffel Tower in Paris. I've also brought our Eurostar tickets from that date. You can see we travelled together, and the photo definitely shows a loving couple."

Ursula held the photo at arm's length. She pulled her spectacles down her nose, pulled a face and inspected it as if it were an image of Pamela Anderson and Tommy Lee displaying their mutual admiration.

"Just because you're kissing in the photo doesn't mean you're living together as if you were husband and wife." She pushed the photo back across the desk with one straight forefinger.

"Well, we were," I said. "Anyway, this should prove it."

I brandished my trump card. "If you compare our passports, they show we entered America, Tonga and New Zealand on the same dates." I stretched out my arms with my palms up. "We've done everything together for the last two years."

Ursula flicked through Fiona's New Zealand passport, placed a stapler on it to wedge it open and unfolded my British passport. She lay them adjacent to each other. "Thank you. I can see you passed through the borders of those countries together. But that doesn't prove you're a couple. You could've been travelling as friends. To consider your application for a partner visa, I need firm proof you've been living together for over a year as if you were married."

I folded my arms and leant back. "But we have. Everyone knows we're in a relationship. What artefacts would satisfy your requirement?"

"Do you have any legal, official documents, addressed to both of you at the same residence over that period? A rental agreement, or bills, or letters from a solicitor? Or could you obtain a signed affidavit from someone in authority who knew you as a de facto married couple in England, and a similar one from a professional in New Zealand? More than one of each if possible?"

"I'm sure I could find someone who'd make a statement. But my visa expires in three weeks. It might take longer than that to receive official letters from England."

Ursula looked at me, sighed, opened her drawer and removed a rubber stamp. She spread my passport with her index and middle fingers and poised the stamp over it in her other hand.

I opened my mouth wide. "No! Don't cancel my visa. I promise I'll get whatever you need."

She frowned and gave a slight head shake. "I'm not cancelling it. I'm granting a two-month bridging permit to allow you time to collate your evidence."

≈ ≈ ≈

Fiona and I lay on our sides in Christchurch's Hagley Park and munched filled rolls. "This immigration thing's such a hassle," she said. "I can't live in England without a visa, and you can't live in New Zealand. I wish we could live together wherever we want and be done with it."

I draped my arm around her shoulder. Spring flowers grew amongst the dappled sunshine, and parents pushed prams along nearby paths.

She lotus-positioned, extracted her diary from her handbag and opened it. "We have until the beginning of February, thanks to the bridging permit. With the delays to the postal service over Christmas we'd better hurry. Who d'you know in England that immigration would consider to be someone in authority?"

"There's the pharmacist in the shop downstairs from our flat?"

"D'you remember his name? Mr Patel, I think. But I'm pretty sure he wouldn't recall us, let alone testify we lived together."

"How about Bob Fletcher, who employed us at the steam fair?"

"I worked there illegally on a tourist visa. I don't want to open that can of worms."

I sat with my head in my hands, then I looked up and pointed one finger. "I know, Doctor Atkins. We attended his surgery as patients, and he'd have the same address on his records for both of us. And he's a person of authority. I'll write to him and ask."

"Great, that takes care of England. What about here?"

I grinned and nodded. "New Zealand's easy."

"Really?"

"Yep. That court case with the Minersville Tavern; the magistrate's a friend of your dad's."

≈ ≈ ≈

Saturday.

Fiona kissed me goodbye, and I began my four-hour drive South in our non-airconditioned car. I sang 'Thank God I'm a Country Boy' to myself, as the route to Haast snaked down the West Coast through remote temperate rain forest, hugging the endless Tasman Sea. I hoped my rendition was good enough for Tom Newell's requirements. An occasional car or milk tanker passed, and I grinned as we exchanged the West Coast salute.

The young lady at the Franz Josef Glacier township coffee shop looked up from her magazine and smiled.

"D'you sell any food for lunch?" I asked.

She flicked her frizzy dark-brown hair away from her face. "I have a couple of sandwiches. Ham or cheese."

"Ham, please, and a coffee."

I perched on a stool opposite her counter. No other customers demanded her attention.

She brought my food and coffee.

"Could I ask you a question?" I said.

"Sure."

"Is there anywhere in Franz Josef which puts on bands?"

She held one fingertip flat to her mouth. "There's the Cook's Saddle Café at Fox, but I haven't seen live music in Franz."

"Oh, okay. I'm a musician, travelling from Hokitika to Haast. I've heard overseas backpackers stay here in the summer to visit the glaciers; it'd be good to play to a younger crowd."

She leant on her arms towards me, cupped her chin in her hands and fluttered her eyelashes. "Goodness, yes. What type of music d'you play?"

"Something for everybody, but I rarely have a chance to perform modern songs I enjoy, by bands such as The Verve, the Red Hot Chili Peppers, Nirvana."

"Wow, d'you play new music? The groups I've seen on the Coast churn out the same old golden oldies and country and western. You should chat with Tiny."

"Tiny?"

"He's the landlord of Batson's Tavern, in the back street here." She pointed with her bare arm. "I work the bar there on weekends. He's never had a band, but you could pop around and tell him Jess thinks you'd be great. I'd love it if you played there. He serves loads of young European backpackers, and I'd persuade all my friends to come too."

"Thanks, Jess, I will." I paused. "Why do they call him Tiny?"

"You'll see."

I finished my coffee and strolled around to Batson's.

≈ ≈ ≈

The tavern stood by itself; a single-storey, red-brick, rectangular building with windows on three sides and a double glass entrance door.

A young man with long, black hair switched off a vacuum cleaner to address me. "We don't open until six, sorry."

"No problem. I'm here to see Tiny."

"Oh, okay. He'll be out the back." He swept his arm. "Straight through the bar."

I stepped over his vacuum hose as he recommenced cleaning, walked behind the counter and entered a storage area which smelt strongly of beer. A rear door opened onto a gravelled yard, where the widest human rear end I'd ever encountered eclipsed the scene in front of me.

Its owner stood up and turned around. In each hand he carried a metal beer keg, swinging either side of his space-hopper tummy. He saw me and set down the barrels.

"Hi, would you be Tiny?" I said. I looked up at him.

"I am."

He held out a hand the size of a tree branch. I shook some of it.

"I'm Simon Michael Prior. I'm a musician from Hokitika. Well, from London, originally. Jess told me I should chat with you about whether I could entertain your customers over the summer."

Tiny pressed his lips together and shook his head slowly. "I've never employed entertainment. We're a small pub, and there's not enough space."

"I'm a one-man band, if you'll pardon the expression. I don't take up much room."

Tiny looked down at me and laughed. "No, you don't look like you do."

"And," I said, "I play all the modern music the backpackers enjoy. Jess said your young European customers would appreciate my performance, as all the other bands play golden oldies."

He ducked under the door into the bar. I followed him.

"Leave me your phone number," he said, "and I'll think about it. Perhaps we could do something in the New Year."

"All right, Tiny. I hope to hear from you."

≈ ≈ ≈

The road meandered further south from Franz Josef, across winding bluffs, through the small glacier township of Fox, bisecting minuscule settlements housing a handful of people: Bruce Bay, Paringa, Jacob's River. Four hours' travel from Hokitika, I entered the little town of Haast, and followed a right turn signposted to Okuru. This road was untouched territory for me, and I slowed down as I drove through the dense forest. A gentle left bend in the road cleaved the route away from the beach, where I came across multiple four-wheel drives and pickup trucks parked on both road verges, and behind them, the chequered motif of a New Zealand police cruiser.

Why are the police all the way out here? Has there been an accident?

I pulled in behind the police car, and saw a cream, wooden building isolated at the side of the road under its red, sagging, corrugated-iron roof. Rhododendron-sized weeds grew up the property, and rust-brown water stains ran down its exterior. A huge, unkempt flax plant guarded the front door. Four schoolroom-like windows were propped open to air the building, but no lights shone from inside.

Is this the right place?

I watched people carry boxes and trays. A lady grasped a flock of multi-coloured helium balloons, each of which announced '50' in white writing. Two men, one in police uniform, knelt by a grey metal cabinet mounted on the ground outside the hall. I stepped out of my car and approached them.

"Hello, is this the Okuru Hall? I'm looking for Tom Newell."

The man not in police attire pushed down on the ground and stood up with some difficulty. "I'm Tom. How can I help?"

His belt strained to retain his trousers, and his ruddy red face suggested a country life well lived.

"I'm Simon Michael Prior, the musician you booked for tonight."

Tom sighed. "G'day, Simon. Thanks for driving all this way. We've encountered a minor problem. You might not be playing at all."

24. RIVER DEEP—MOUNTAIN HIGH

"Pardon? I might not be playing at all? Have I driven all this way for nothing?"

Tom threw his hands in the air and shook his head. "As you'll have realised, this hall's rather remote. I don't think anyone's rented it for over a year."

The policeman glanced over his shoulder. "I don't think anyone's paid the power bill for over a year either. Tom, can you reach in the back of the Holden and grab the orange toolbox?"

"No problem, Mark."

I watched Tom walk over to the police car and open the boot. Meanwhile, Officer Mark poked a small brush inside the metal cabinet and swept out decades of spiders' webs and dead weeds. Tom returned with the police tool box, and Mark rummaged for a screwdriver and a torch. He shone light into the cabinet, lay the torch down and turned his head over his shoulder.

"Does anyone have a length of stiff wire?"

"Would a guitar string do?" I asked. "Give me a minute."

I grabbed my guitar case, flipped it open and pulled out an old E string. The policeman unravelled it.

"That's not thick enough. D'you have anything else?"

"Umm, I have a power lead. Hang on."

I tipped my bag of cables onto the grass as if I'd accidentally emptied a pan of black spaghetti down the sink, tugged one end of a cord and gave it to the policeman.

"D'you need this?" he asked.

"If it means the difference between the party going ahead, or not, you'd better have it."

Mark extracted a pair of snippers and chopped off a foot of cable. His powerful hands spliced it into three strands. He sliced a length of yellow core and stripped the insulation from its ends with his teeth. "Tom, can you hold the torch? I should wear gloves for the next part."

He retrieved a pair of thick, black gloves from a pouch around his waist. Tom pointed the torch into the metal box while Mark reached in with his screwdriver in one hand and my yellow cable in the other.

"Nearly done. Tom, shine it here, would you?"

Tom shone the light, Mark turned the screwdriver, and to our left the hall illuminated. I placed my hand over my heart and breathed out.

Tom slapped the policeman's back. "Great job, Mark." He turned to me. "Simon, d'you want to bring your gear in and set up on the stage?"

I realised I had just observed the Mayor of Haast and the local policeman bypass the electricity meter at a public building, and knew there were some things about the West Coast I absolutely loved.

The policeman brushed grass off his legs. "Tom," he said, "I'm off duty at ten o'clock. If your guests plan to do anything stupid, can you make sure they finish it by then so I can enjoy a beer with you?"

≈ ≈ ≈

Partygoers of all ages thronged the hall as I bounded on stage. Some had dressed smartly for the occasion; others appeared to have arrived directly from working on dairy farms or fishing boats. Tom held court at the back of the room, shaking hands with men, kissing ladies, patting children on the head. A huge, circular cake with fifty candles rested on a table in front of me. I figured no-one would push his face in it tonight.

I can't believe how many people he knows. I'm honoured to be here.

Barely any room remained as people ate, drank, danced and cheered. Tom gave me a big thumbs up and clapped above his head when I started the first verse of 'Thank God I'm a Country Boy'.

At 10.30 a lady brandishing a Canon waved her whole arm at me as I belted out the last verse of 'Great Balls of Fire'. "Could you take a break while we do the speeches? Feel free to grab some food."

A middle-aged man ascended the three steps to the stage and introduced himself as Tom's brother. He spoke into my microphone and rattled off a series of reminiscences about their youth growing up in the area, and Tom smiled and studied his shoes. The food table bowed under several plates of party snacks, so I grabbed a beer and a paper plate and selected a pie, a sausage roll and what looked like tinned asparagus spears wrapped in cheap, white bread; a delicacy I'd never considered could exist in a civilised world.

A girl of about my age helped herself to a pastry. She smiled at me and paused with it halfway to her mouth. "Hi. You're from London, right?"

I couldn't place her accent. "Yes, I'm Simon." I set down my beer and shook the hand that didn't contain the pastry.

"My name's Stacy," she said. "I'm from Newcastle. The Newcastle in the north of England." She had a long, brown ponytail, and wore no make-up on her sun-reddened cheeks.

"Wow," I said. "You're a long way from home. What brings you here?"

She laughed. "I could say the same about you. My boyfriend's a local; we met in England when he worked on my uncle's farm. His British visa ran out, and I decided to come and live here with him on the Coast."

Laughter reverberated around the hall as Tom's brother recounted another episode.

"It's the same story with me," I said. "My girlfriend's from Hokitika. How long have you lived in Haast?"

"Two years. I love it here. Life's more relaxed than in the UK. And no crime. I park the car outside the pub and leave the keys in it. Can you imagine doing that in Newcastle? It'd be gone before you turned your back."

I paused as a thought crossed my mind. "Which New Zealand visa d'you have, Stacy?"

"When I arrived, I had a one-year working holiday permit, but I managed to change it to a partner de facto one."

"Fiona and I are suffering with that immigration process at the moment. We assembled what we considered to be sufficient evidence of our relationship, but the lady rejected it and asked for signed affidavits and legal documents."

"A man interviewed us," said Stacy. "I had to wait outside his office as he asked my boyfriend personal questions, which people who live together would know. For instance, the colour of my toothbrush, which food I enjoyed or disliked, and my favourite TV program. Then he asked me the same questions while Shaun stood in the corridor."

She shook her head. "I thought they'd rejected us. I mean, who remembers what colour toothbrush their partner had a year ago? Ridiculous."

I pinched my lips and nodded. "Yep, ridiculous."

"Anyway," said Stacy. "They gave me the de facto visa, and next year I'll be eligible to apply for citizenship and a New Zealand passport and stay here forever."

"And what about your partner? Is he pleased to be back?"

"Yes, he's devoted to his family. Plus, he's a country boy. He becomes nervous if he sees a traffic light."

We both laughed as a lady touched my arm. "Sorry, Simon. Could you play 'Happy Birthday to You' please? They're about to cut the cake."

"Sure." I turned back to Stacy. "Nice to meet you, and thanks for the tips about toothbrushes and things."

She grinned and gave me a thumbs up. "Good luck with the visa."

I pushed through the audience and stepped back onto the stage.

≈ ≈ ≈

"Wasn't it a fantastic party last night?" said the receptionist, as I checked out of the Haast hotel. "I reckon Tom would've been overjoyed with your music."

"Oh, were you at the hall? Sorry, so many people attended I don't recognise everyone."

I watched a deluge cascade down the outside of the hotel window. "Now to start the long drive back up the coast to Hokitika."

"Take care out there," she said. "The rain's torrential, and the rivers'll be in flood."

"I will, thanks."

I handed her my key as someone tapped my shoulder. A white-haired man dressed in a tweed jacket and rumpled trousers stood behind me. "Excuse me?" he said. "Are you London Musician Simon Michael Prior?" He wore a Doctor Who scarf, and spectacles dangled on a chain from his neck.

I nodded and wondered what he wanted. "I am Simon Michael Prior, yes."

"When I arrived, the receptionist informed me another Prior had checked in. My name's Ian Prior."

I grinned and shook his hand. "Nice to meet you, Mr Prior."

It feels odd to say that.

"I'm on holiday from Wellington. If you're ever visiting the capital, please look me up and come and stay."

"Thank you. How will I find your address?"

"Easy. Open any copy of the phone book. I'm the only Prior in Wellington. What a pleasure to bump into you; it's rare that I encounter a fellow Prior."

I shook the hand of a complete stranger who'd invited me to stay at his home based solely on our shared surname, and realised I liked New Zealand very much indeed.

≈ ≈ ≈

Rushing, dirty water splashed against the underside of the elongated, single-lane bridge spanning the Haast river. I glanced over the edge, gripped the wheel and accelerated. If the torrent overflowed, I didn't want to be caught driving across it. The windscreen wipers vibrated at top speed but couldn't compete with the downpour, so I reduced the car's speed to forty kilometres per hour. Not a single vehicle approached me or overtook me. Lush trees darkened the road, and I flicked on my high beam. I bit my nails.

Two hours.

Two hours until the safety of the next significant town.

Am I the only driver crazy enough to travel in this?

The rain eased, and I increased speed to sixty. Still well below the limit, but as fast as I dared to drive. The tiny hamlets of Paringa and Bruce Bay blurred past in the mist, and I still hadn't seen a soul.

A sign announced the few houses which made up Jacob's River settlement, then tail lights glowed ahead of me, and I pumped the brakes.

How can there be a traffic jam in this place? We're in the middle of nowhere.

I wound down my window and leant out to peer around the line of campervans but couldn't see any reason for the queue. Five minutes passed and nothing moved. The rain stopped, so I stepped out of the car and walked. At the front of the line, the reason for the problem became apparent. A muddy, brown flow surged across the road, and uprooted trees pushed against the Jacob's River bridge rails as white water sluiced around them. On the opposite side of the torrent, a similar queue of traffic fronted by a tour bus stretched into the distance. I put my hands in my pockets and gazed across the whirlpooling flood water separating me from my home and Fiona. No gauge showed depth, and none of the tourists dared drive through.

A man in a heavy green raincoat and Wellington boots approached me.

"Now what do we do?" I asked him.

"Are you a local?" he asked. "You don't look like a loopy."

I recalled the West Coast residents' moniker for tourists. "I'm from Hokitika. Why?"

"You've a couple of options. Either you turn around and spend two days travelling back to Haast, across the pass to Wanaka, up through the Mackenzie district and over the mountains again via Arthur's, or you attempt what Kaye's doing." He pointed across the river, and I observed an elderly, red Toyota station wagon plough through the water slowly with a bow wave preceding it. My jaw hung open as I tracked the vehicle's progress. At one point, my eyes convinced me the force of the river had pushed it sideways, and I covered my mouth with my hand. The car exited the current, and the driver wound down her window.

"Morning, Paul." She revealed a crooked, stained smile with one front tooth absent, and her hair didn't seem to have collided with a brush for decades.

"G'day, Kaye. Bit wet today."

I stepped forward. "Excuse me? I'm trying to make my way home to Hokitika. D'you reckon I could drive through like you did?"

"What car d'you have?" asked Kaye. She leant out of the window with one green-jacketed elbow.

"A Honda Prelude."

"That's a bit low to the ground, but you'll be fine. Remain on the upstream side, stay in second gear, keep your revs high and your speed slow, and whatever you do, don't change into third while you're in the water. I have to go, sorry. I need to check on the animals. Good luck."

I returned to my car. Most of the tourists had headed back towards Haast, and I discovered it abandoned and alone. Paul directed operations as I approached.

"Hang on. Make sure no-one's coming the other way." He stretched his neck to see to the opposite side. "You're good. Off you go."

I clenched my teeth and engaged second gear.

I'm a local.

I'm not a tourist.

I'm not a loopy.

I can do this.

I heard the engine race as water splashed in front of the bonnet. Immediately, the force of the flood shoved me to the left.

Downstream.

Towards the sea.

25. NEW YEAR'S DAY

I turned my steering wheel to the right and clenched it until my knuckles whitened.

I do not die today. This is not where it ends.

I expected river water to enter via the door sills but it didn't.

Windows down.

High revs.

Don't change gear.

A tree branch banged against my bonnet, spun around and headed downstream.

Halfway. Come on, come on.

The water subsided.

Quick, quick.

Steam billowed from the engine as I accelerated out of the river and passed tourists waiting beside the stranded bus. One Nikoned my exit as I waved, changed up to third gear, and headed for home.

≈ ≈ ≈

Fiona ran from our hut and squeezed me. "I worried you'd never return. The news shows floods and landslips all along the Coast."

I grinned and spun her around. "Jacob's River almost wiped me out but I made it."

We walked inside and shut the door.

"How did Tom Newell's party go?" she asked.

"Brilliant. I reckon the whole of Haast attended."

She laughed. "About one hundred people then."

"I'm sure over a hundred turned up, so goodness knows where they came from. Anyway, I met this nice English girl there called Stacy."

Fiona folded her arms. "Oh, yes?"

I grinned and rubbed her shoulder. "She told me she'd been granted the partner visa we're applying for. They interviewed her and her partner separately and asked them all sorts of personal questions: the colour of their toothbrushes, their favourite dinners, their favourite TV shows."

Fiona shrugged. "I've no idea what colour your toothbrush is, and I must see it every day."

"We won't have to be accurate, so long as our answers are both the same. We should invest some time in preparation."

≈ ≈ ≈

The warmth of the summer's day allowed us to prop the kitchen door open, and I smiled while I constructed a ham and salad sandwich and listened to calves mooing in the opposite paddock.

"What's the plan for Christmas?"

Linda immersed her hands in the washing up water and addressed me over her shoulder. "The same as last year. Family comes around; we eat turkey, drink beer or wine, polish off one of Nana's trifles and milk the cows in the afternoon. D'you have any gigs arranged over the holiday period?"

"I'm performing at the Hari Hari Motor Inn on Christmas Eve. The manager said he's fully booked with tourists, so he wants some entertainment to keep them spending money in the bar."

Linda wiped her hands on a tea towel and flipped a calendar. "Christmas day's on Thursday this year."

"Then on New Year's Eve, Gary's employed me, at the Kokatahi Pub just down the road. Why don't you both come along? It should be a great night."

"What d'you reckon, Frank?" asked Linda. "If Simon's playing locally, we won't have far to drive home."

Frank lowered the paper and puffed out his cheeks. "It's been years since I've stayed awake 'til midnight. I'm normally in bed by nine."

"I'll tell you what," I said. "If you come to the pub on New Year's Eve, I'll buy you a whisky."

He turned to me and grinned. "Whisky? Well, in that case.."

≈ ≈ ≈

The familiar smell of cigarette smoke and stale drinks entered my nostrils as I watched the landlord of the Kokatahi pub transfer boxes of beer bottles from a back room into the bar. He set down a crate on the floor, stood up and wiped his forehead.

"G'day, Simon. It's hot, isn't it? How are you today?" His walrus moustache wiggled as he smiled.

"Well, thanks, Gary. Are you stocking up?"

"Yep. We normally can't find a band on New Year's Eve prepared to travel out here, but with you being local, it's all worked out well. I'm expecting the entire valley to attend."

I bounced on my tiptoes. "I can't wait, Gary. We'll all know each other, and I can have a few drinks myself. It'll be one big happy party." I glanced around the empty pub. "Where shall I set up?"

"Over there, in front of the window." Gary pointed to the back wall. "Excuse me, I'd better keep going. People'll start arriving soon."

≈ ≈ ≈

By nine o'clock, groups of farmers and their families stood in small circles holding beer and wine glasses. Sweat dripped down my face as I sang, and I mopped it with my sleeve. Several people greeted me as I performed a selection of background music, and they didn't seem to realise I only possessed one mouth and I wasn't able to sing and converse with them simultaneously.

"It's three hours until the big event. My name's London Musician Simon Michael Prior, although..," I glanced around the crowd, "most of you know me as Simon. I'll take a brief break and return in a few minutes." I unshouldered my guitar and popped to the toilet.

A young man stood at the next urinal. I recognised his face but couldn't place him.

"Hi, Simon," he said. "D'you remember me? You played at my 21st, back in May?"

I smiled at him with the awkwardness of two lads standing in close proximity, both with their trouser zips undone. "You're Brandon, right? That party where your friends pushed you in the cake, and the following day the fields were scattered with crashed cars?"

"Yep. Let's hope that doesn't happen tonight." He grinned, and we turned around to the washbasins.

"We normally venture into town for New Year's Eve," said Brandon, "but when we heard you were playing out here in the valley, my friends and I thought we'd drink locally. May I buy you a beer?"

"Thanks; I'd love a cold one."

We exited to the bar.

"What'll you have?"

"A large Lion Brown, please. I need to cool off."

Gary levered the pump and placed the drink in front of me. By the time he'd poured Brandon's beer, I'd finished mine.

"Jeez, you were thirsty," said Gary. I'll bring you another in a minute."

"Thanks, Gary, and thank you, Brandon. I'd better play some more music."

I strode away from the bar, threw on my guitar and launched into 'Brown Eyed Girl'. The second verse contained a brief interruption as Gary placed a jug of beer and an empty glass on top of my amplifier. I watched the surface of the drink vibrate in time to the music and had a random image of a scene from *Jurassic Park*.

≈ ≈ ≈

By 10.30 p.m. my jug of Lion Brown had evaporated again, and I desperately needed the toilet.

"Thank you, ladies and gentlemen; I'll be back shortly." Once I finished in the bathroom, I strolled over to the bar and discovered Fiona chatting with friends. I tapped her on the shoulder.

"Hi," she said. "Are you having fun?"

"I am, thanks. It's great performing when I know so many people." I observed her empty champagne flute. "D'you want another wine?"

"I'd better not," she said. "Someone has to drive."

"What about your parents?"

"Don't let Mum have any more alcohol. She's had three glasses of bubbles and turned all giggly. And I reckon Dad's drunk more than a couple of whiskies."

I glanced behind me and noticed Frank propping up the bar.

"Did you all arrive in the same car?"

"Yep. Dad had to return machinery he'd borrowed from another farmer, so we brought his Honda, and the trailer's attached to the back. Goodness knows how we'll travel home. There's no way Mum or Dad'll be able to drive, and you seem to have had a few."

"Erm, yes. Gary brought me a jug of beer, and it's so hot in here, I'm drinking it like water. Anyway, I'd better say 'hi' to your dad. I'll see you at the end."

Frank slammed his forearm on the bar counter. "Simon, fancy seeing you here." He grinned between two red cheeks.

"Evening, Frank. Are you enjoying yourself?"

He'd dressed in his smartest short-sleeved shirt and trousers, and sweat stains had formed under his arms.

"I am. Gary's looking after me well." He held out an empty glass, and Gary filled it from a bottle with 'Courvoisier' on the label.

"I didn't know you drank Brandy?"

"I don't," said Frank. He sipped the Courvoisier.

Gary held one palm to his side of mouth and leant towards me. "I only had one bottle of whisky in the pub, and he's finished it. He doesn't seem to have noticed."

He placed another jug of beer in front of me. "Here you are. Keep those vocal chords lubricated."

Frank raised his glass and grinned again.

≈ ≈ ≈

One minute to midnight. Farming folk of all ages clapped, cheered and gyrated on a cleared section of carpet. I paused at the end of 'Old Time Rock and Roll'. "Ladies and gentlemen, 1997 is history. In less than a minute, New Zealand will be the first major country in the world to move into 1998. Welcome to the future."

The pub clock's second hand ascended its left-hand side.

I counted like a NASA commentator announcing a Space Shuttle launch, and the pubgoers accompanied me.

"Ten, nine, eight, seven, six, five, four, three, two, one, Happy New Year!"

I launched into a drunken version of 'Auld Lang Syne'. The farmers held hands and formed a circle, then drew together and apart repeatedly. Their actions became considerably more violent each time, until one lad fell over and dragged several others with him, to much laughter. I wondered how many verses 'Auld Lang Syne' needed to contain and figured twenty should be enough.

"Thank you; it's been a fantastic evening. Happy 1998!"

I stumbled to the bar. "Gary, is it all right if I leave my gear here and pick it up tomorrow? We'll all have to squish into my car; Fiona's the only one sober enough to drive."

"No problem. Although, we'd be unlucky if the cops turned up here. I can't remember the last time they did. Someone would have rung the pub and told me if they were waiting outside."

Fiona collected her parents. Linda grasped an empty wine glass and Frank reminded me of a Coca-Cola Father Christmas, with rosy cheeks and twinkling eyes.

"Come on," said Fiona. "I'll drive you all home."

"No, you won't," said Frank.

26. PUMP UP THE VOLUME

Frank gripped the bar to ensure it didn't collapse without his support. "I'm fine to take my car. Plus, the trailer's on the back, and I need it tomorrow."

Fiona inspected her father and fixed her hands on her hips. "Dad, you're not sober enough to walk, let alone drive."

Frank waved the back of his hand twice. "Don't worry about me. I've been driving for over fifty years. What could possibly go wrong?"

He pulled his car keys from his pocket and turned them over as if he hadn't expected to discover them there.

"I'm riding with Fiona," said Linda. "If you want to end up in a ditch that's your decision, but you can do it by yourself."

"All right, Dad," said Fiona. "We'll follow directly behind, to ensure you make it home in one piece."

"I don't know what you're worried about," said Frank. "I've hardly had anything to drink." He walked towards the exit, pausing briefly to collide with a table.

The cool night air slapped my cheeks as soon as we stepped outside, and I immediately felt more sober. "Quick," I said. "Hop in the car. Frank's already started his engine."

I watched Frank's car and trailer perform a dramatic semi-circle in the gravel car park and bump into the road.

Fiona spun her tyres, and we headed after him.

"Bloody hell," said Linda. "He's driving at over one hundred kilometres per hour."

We chased after Frank in a scene straight from *The Spy Who Loved Me*.

"Far out, Dad took the corner at seventy," said Fiona. "I can't keep up."

She sped up as the red lights of Frank's trailer vanished into the distance. I floundered from left to right in the back seat. We bounced through potholes along the farm driveway, and our headlights reflected in the cloud of dust Frank's car created.

Linda gritted her teeth and grasped the passenger door handle. "He's going to drive straight through the bloody garage if he doesn't slow down."

Frank's brake lights glowed, and we illuminated him as he slammed his car door and wobbled into the farmhouse. Linda jumped out of our car and followed. I shrugged. Fiona and I closed our car doors. She threw her arms around my neck and kissed me in the way she didn't in front of her parents.

"Happy New Year, Simon. I wonder what adventures we'll have in 1998."

I held her waist. "I can't wait for another year with you."

We walked towards our hut.

"Hang on a moment," I said. "I want to check something."

I entered the darkness of Frank's garage and sidled along the edge of his car. The Honda's engine *tic-tic-ticked* as it cooled down. I arrived at the front of the car and felt the edge of the bonnet.

Frank had halted with one inch to spare.

≈ ≈ ≈

TAP TAP TAP TAP TAP

Go away.

TAP TAP TAP

Please…

TAP TAP

For goodness' sake..

I lifted my head, pulled back the curtains and found Linda standing outside in her dressing gown.

She raised her hands to her mouth and shouted through the closed window. "Phone call for you, Simon. Someone called Tony?"

My head throbbed and my eyes swam as I tugged on sweaty New Year's Eve clothes and bent down to tie up shoes. I ran over to the farmhouse and held onto the kitchen worktop to relieve the head spins.

Linda spoke into the receiver. "Hang on, Tony, he's coming."

"Hello?"

"Simon, it's Tiny."

I furrowed my brow.

Tiny? Tiny.. ah, yes.

"Tiny, from Franz Josef? How are you?"

"Great, thanks. Jess keeps asking for music, so I dug out your number. Could you come down next Friday? It's her birthday on the weekend, and a good excuse for a party."

At last. No more Cliff Richard and Kenny Rogers.

"No problem. What time d'you want me to start?"

"I'd say nine p.m., and keep going until one in the morning, or whenever the last person collapses. You won't want to drive home at that time, so I'll book you into the hostel."

"Sounds great, Tiny. I'm looking forward to this."

≈ ≈ ≈

Jess juggled pint glasses, money and till buttons. Young people waved bank notes across the bar, and I discerned German, English and Spanish accents. I grinned as I estimated the average age of the customers to be around 21.

Tiny wiped his hands on a cloth far too small to contain them. "G'day, Simon. Where d'you reckon you could set up?"

"How about beside the fire? You won't be using it in summer, so I could spread across it and be less obtrusive."

He slapped me on the back and knocked the wind out of me. "Sounds good. D'you want something to eat? There's a menu around here somewhere." He handed me a laminated card with four options on it. I chose a Kiwi burger and chips.

Jess noticed me and waved. "Hi, Simon." She clenched her fists in front of her and grinned. "I was so excited when Tiny said he'd booked you. I can't wait to have a boogie, if these customers allow me a spare moment."

"Tiny mentioned it's your birthday?"

"Yep. 22 on Sunday." She pulled a beer and slid it towards me.

I raised my glass to her. "Happy Birthday for Sunday, Jess. Is there any favourite song I can play for you?"

"D'you play Oasis?"

"Sure do."

"Great. 'Wonderwall', please. I can't stop, sorry. I'll catch you later." She smiled and blew me a kiss.

I squashed my equipment into the fireplace. The chef placed my burger and chips on a small table with cutlery tightly rolled in a paper napkin.

"Here's your order." His chest puffed out. "I'm Richard. I'm the head chef."

I reckon you're the only chef.

"Hi, Richard. We met briefly last year. You were vacuuming. I'm Simon, the musician tonight."

Richard scratched his head. "Where are you from? You don't speak English the same as we do."

"I'm from London, originally."

"London? Is that an actual place?"

"I beg your pardon? What d'you mean—is it an actual place?"

"I always thought London was like *Star Trek*. Something you saw on TV, but not real. I didn't realise people came from there."

I hoped Richard was joking, not least because he worked in a pub frequented primarily by foreigners. He didn't seem to be the shiniest bauble on the tree.

"I'm sure it's real, Richard. My dad lives there, so I bloody hope it is."

Richard laughed. "I reckon you're from Christchurch. I think you're pulling my chain."

"Um, okay.."

≈ ≈ ≈

9.00.

I pushed through the crowd of twenty-somethings to reach my guitar. I hoped they'd be able to hear the music above the conversation in more tongues than a European Parliamentary debate.

I struck a chord. "Welcome to Franz Josef, on the wonderful West Coast of New Zealand. I'm Simon Michael Prior, and I'll be entertaining you tonight. Here's a special song for the lovely lady behind the bar serving your drinks tonight; she'll be 22 on Sunday. Happy Birthday, Jess."

I launched into 'Wonderwall'. Jess grinned and waved her spare fist high in the air while her other hand held a glass under a beer tap.

An impromptu dancefloor formed in the centre of the pub. As more and more people joined in, it enlarged until every table and chair ended up stacked against the walls. Young chaps with long hair and beards danced with bleached-blonde, tanned girls wearing tank tops and Daisy Duke denim shorts. Everyone became best friends instantly. There would be no chance to play background music tonight, thank goodness. I'd dug a six-foot deep trench and filled it with country and western singers. I planted my feet wide apart and reached to my left to turn up the volume.

'Smells Like Teen Spirit' followed 'Wonderwall', 'Friday I'm in Love' followed 'Bitter Sweet Symphony'. 'Parklife' followed 'Come Out and Play'. Tiny marched to the double doors and locked them, as the pub capacity reached critical level. I noticed two young chaps force a window open from the outside and squeeze through. The floor bounced beneath me, and airborne beer sloshed onto the ceiling as I powered through the first chords of 'Blister in the Sun'.

Jess shoved through the throng to clear glasses. She brought me another drink and pointed at Tiny, who leant heavily on the end of the bar. "He's had too many beers," she shouted. "Anything could happen now."

I wondered what volume of alcohol someone his size would need to drink before their body noticed. Tiny steamrolled through the crowd. He plucked my microphone from its stand and raised it to his lips. I paused in the middle of the Violent Femmes' song and gave him room to make whatever announcement was about to come out.

Tiny took a deep breath like an industrial vacuum cleaner. "Right, you lot. Listen up."

The backpackers stopped and looked at him. He stared around the room to ensure he had their attention. I grimaced and hoped he wouldn't announce the night had ended and the bar was closed.

He cleared his throat. "Everybody…"

One hundred young tourists anticipated his forthcoming utterances.

"Free drinks for anyone not wearing a top. Boys and girls."

He grinned and stepped away from the microphone, as a stampede of drunken backpackers pulled their T-shirts and singlets over their heads.

≈ ≈ ≈

Jess collected glasses and squared tables for the following day's service. Tiny gathered empty bottles and clinked them into a black rubbish sack. Richard swept broken glass, as I switched off my amplifier and coiled my cables.

"Thanks for the best birthday ever," said Jess. "You're so good. I loved every song."

"My pleasure, Jess. I had a great night too."

She paused and touched my arm. "Simon, d'you have a girlfriend?"

27. DON'T YOU WANT ME

I pulled back, and Jess removed her hand.

"Sorry, Jess, I do have a girlfriend. She's called Fiona, and we live together in Hokitika."

She rolled her eyes and stacked glasses in the crook of her arm. "Why are all the best ones taken?"

Richard leant on his broom, displayed a wide toothy grin like the 'before' picture for dental brace treatment, and opened his eyes wide. "I'm not taken."

"No, Richard," said Jess. "You're not."

Tiny dropped his sack, threw his head back and laughed.

≈ ≈ ≈

Hokitika town centre on a summer lunchtime.

Warm.

Humid.

Busy.

Tour buses sneezed air brakes. Visitors meandered along the pavements, in and out of shops, purchasing mantelpiece-adorning dust-collecting jade ornaments, blown glass and hand-carved wooden bowls. Waiting staff brought coffees and sandwiches and cleared empty plates and cups.

I jumped the stairs two at a time to Mike Keenan's office, sprang through his open door and immediately stopped. Dennis Stark sat opposite Mike at his desk. He leant back in his chair with his hands behind his back, and the bottom of his bare tummy peeked from under his shirt.

The one man I never want to see again in my life.

I took a deep breath. "Sorry, Mike, I didn't realise you had company. I'll pop back later."

"It's okay, Simon. This is Dennis; he's from the council."

"I know," I said, "we've met."

I smiled thinly at Dennis, who nodded minutely and picked his nose.

"How can I help?" asked Mike.

"Erm, I wondered whether you'd considered my application to appear at the Wild Foods Festival?"

Dennis sat forward, and his belly drooped to fill the void between his open legs. "Has this tosser applied to play at the festival?"

"Err, Simon has enquired, yes," said Mike. "He's a local chap, y'know."

Dennis stood and placed his knuckles on Mike's desk. "There is no way this pommie bastard's going to play at the Wild Foods Festival. He's crap."

His face took on a buddleia-coloured hue, and he faced Mike while prodding his finger at me. "A chap I know at Brunner Working Mens' Club said nobody turned up to see him at all. And at another place, someone hated his playing so much, they tried to dynamite the pub. And, and…," his finger jabbed more enthusiastically, "..one pub landlord refused to pay him because of all the swearing, and that ended up in court."

Mike held out his upturned hands. "Come on, Dennis. I heard Simon won that case."

Dennis thumped the desk. "I don't care who bloody won it. He's bad for publicity and I'm not risking the good name of the Wild Foods Festival by allowing him anywhere near it."

He waved dismissively and marched out.

I heard his heavy footsteps clump down the stairs.

Mike cleared his throat and shuffled papers. He glanced down and avoided my gaze. "Erm, perhaps you could apply next year, Simon?"

I stood with my mouth open and felt the tops of my cheeks burn. A quiet voice which didn't sound like mine answered him.

"All right, Mike. Thanks, anyway."

I swivelled and shuffled out.

The first tears came when I reached the street.

≈ ≈ ≈

Fiona draped her arm around my shoulder. I sat with my lips pinched, and I whacked the kitchen table, causing the dinner cutlery to briefly become airborne.

"I can't believe it. I've worked so hard for this. They can't take it from me."

Fiona rubbed my back. "I'm so sorry. Dennis Stark's an idiot. Everything's always personal with him."

"That's the trouble in a small town," said Linda. "If someone takes a dislike to you, they can make your life very difficult."

Frank sat silently with his head back, his eyes closed and one finger flat on his mouth. He stood up, opened the phone book, stretched the telephone cable into the hall and closed the door. We heard his voice, but we couldn't distinguish the words. He returned a moment later.

"What was that call about?" asked Linda. "It can't have been your bookie; they're closed at this time."

"Nothing important, Linda," said Frank. "Nothing important. Someone I remembered I needed to ring."

Linda picked up her knife and fork and gave him a glance which demonstrated she didn't believe him at all.

≈ ≈ ≈

I slumped on the outdoor step and stared between my feet. Jazz lay by my side and inspected me by lifting one eyebrow at a time. Phillip strolled past.

"Everything okay?" he asked. "D'you want to help me fix some fences?"

"Sure. No problem. Anything to take my mind off things."

"What's happened?"

"I wanted to play music at the Wild Foods Festival, and I'd convinced myself I'd be guaranteed a spot because I'm a local. But it seems that isn't the case."

Phillip removed his baseball cap.

"They can be a funny bunch here. If you rub up certain people the wrong way, you're doomed. We call it tall poppy syndrome. If one poppy grows taller than the others, it has to be chopped down. It's prevalent in small town New Zealand. I remember this chap we called Cowboy; he ran a business selling mail-order American wild west gear. Someone on the council didn't appreciate his success, and they made life more and more difficult for him. First, they banned him from having a sandwich board at the corner of the street, then they objected to advertisements in his window and eventually it all became too hard for him, and he skipped town and set up somewhere else."

"That someone on the council who took a dislike to Cowboy, it wasn't Dennis Stark, was it?"

"No idea. Could've been any of them."

≈ ≈ ≈

We returned to the farmhouse for afternoon tea.

"You received a phone call while you were out on the farm," said Linda. "Athol Olsen."

"Athol Olsen? I don't recognise the name. D'you know him?"

"Vaguely. I see him in town sometimes. He always wears a leather, broad-brimmed hat. I've no idea what he'd want with you. Here's the number."

I picked up the receiver and dialled. "Athol Olsen? Simon Michael Prior, returning your call."

"Simon, thanks for calling back. I organise the Westland Agricultural and Pastoral show. It's held down at the Hokitika racecourse on the last Saturday in January. There are several attractions during the afternoon. Cattle and sheep judging, a tug of war, firefighters, a guide dog demonstration, a beautiful baby competition, and so on."

"Sounds interesting. How can I help?"

"It's a big event; we attract a few thousand people. I wondered if you'd do us the honour of playing some music on stage, in between the events as the next performance sets up?"

I opened my mouth wide, and my eyebrows climbed to the top of my head.

Yes! This is going to be it. A proper, outdoor, stadium gig.

"Of course I could. Give me the details of the program on the day, and I'll fit around you. Thanks, Athol. Wow, I'm looking forward to it."

I bounced into the dining room. Fiona, Frank and Linda drank tea and ate home baking.

I pulled Fiona from her chair, picked her up and spun her around.

"Ow. Put me down. What's all this about?"

I deposited her back in her seat, locked my fingers together and stretched my arms above my head. "You'll never guess what's happened?"

"Go on," said Fiona.

Frank lowered his newspaper and let his glasses dangle on a chain.

"This Athol Olsen chap hired me to play the Westland Agricultural and Pastoral show. One of the biggest events in Hokitika."

"Seriously?" said Linda. "I don't think I've seen bands there in previous years."

Fiona grinned at me. "You'll be so pleased, after your disappointment with the Wild Foods Festival."

I bounced from left foot to right foot and waved my arms in the air. "I need to buy new guitar strings. And some more plectrums. And fix my microphone stand; it's held together with tape." The carpet scruggled up as I spun in a circle on the spot.

Frank smiled to himself, replaced his glasses and disappeared back into the paper.

≈ ≈ ≈

A hot wind blew in Christchurch. Gritty dust sandstormed along the pavements and forced pedestrians to turn their heads sideways as they walked. Fiona shoved open the door to the immigration office, and we climbed the stairs to wait in the reception area. I grasped my pack of evidence documents and bit my nails.

"Quick recap," said Fiona. "What colour toothbrush did I own in London?"

"Blue. What colour was mine?"

"White. What was my favourite dinner?"

"Erm, spaghetti Bolognese?"

"Yep, and yours was Mexican fajitas."

"Correct."

Fiona smoothed her skirt down. "My favourite TV show?"

"I can't remember. *Coronation Street?*"

"Far out, I've never watched *Coronation Street*. Try again. I remember you hated it."

I cupped my chin in my hand and tapped my finger on my cheek. "I know. That cringe-worthy, dreadful presenter. What was it called? Hang on."

I held one finger up. "Got it. *All Rise for Julian Clary*."

"Well done. And yours was that police program, *The Bill*. She probably won't ask us any of those questions now."

The white door swung open, and Ursula inspected Fiona and me. A flicker of recognition crossed her face. "Good morning," she said. "Please come in."

We sat in two chairs before her desk. Ursula opened the top drawer of a grey filing cabinet and clawed the hanging files backwards and forwards.

"Bear with me for a minute."

I jiggled and tapped my fingers.

"Sit still," whispered Fiona.

She took my hand, encountered the squishy sweat in my palm and immediately released it.

Ursula found the file she needed, manoeuvred herself behind the desk, spread it in front of her and flicked through it page by page. My heart thumped against the inside of my chest. She peered at me over her glasses and cleared her throat.

"We met in November, I recall, and you applied for a partner visa, based on the assumption you'd been living together as if you were husband and wife for..," she referred to the file in front of her, "..two years."

I tried to say, "that's correct," but my voice escalated several octaves. I coughed and repeated it.

Ursula continued. "And you're still living together?"

I sat on my hands and wiggled from side to side. "Yes, we are."

She glanced at Fiona, then at me. I tried to remember the name of Fiona's favourite television show, but my nerves had dumped it in the rubbish bin of terror, and I hoped she didn't reach that part of her interrogation.

"What have you brought for me to review?"

"Erm, you asked for affidavits from people in authority, stating they knew us as a de facto married couple."

Ursula leant back in her chair and folded her arms. "Well? Have you obtained these affidavits?"

I pulled a piece of paper out of my envelope, rotated it and pushed it across the table. "This is from a magistrate on the West Coast. It states he's known us as a cohabiting couple since December 1996."

Ursula took the letter, skimmed it, and put it to one side. "D'you have anything else?"

I extracted another document. "Our family doctor signed this, in England. He's affirmed both of us were registered with him since March 1996, and we lived at the same address."

Ursula looked at the letter. She turned it over and back again. She glanced at the bottom of the paper.

"This, Doctor, err.. Atkins. You're right, he's written to say you're both registered with him and living at the same address. But there's nothing to say you're not just flatmates. He doesn't say you're in a cohabiting relationship as if you were a married couple. I don't think I can accept this."

I clenched my jaw and threw my arms up. I was becoming annoyed with this woman, and the power she delighted in holding over us. "Hang on. When we came to see you in November last year, we told you we'd been living in England for over twelve months as a couple. Doctor Atkins' letter might not say exactly that, but surely you can see the intent of his statement? We then travelled through the USA and Tonga together and arrived in New Zealand in December 1996. The proof is the passport stamps we showed you."

I stood up, reached over her desk and tapped my index finger on a piece of paper. "The affidavit from the West Coast magistrate states he's known us as a cohabiting couple for over a year. For goodness' sake, surely all of this evidence meets your criteria?"

I sat down, and my shoulders slumped. Fiona's mouth fell open, and she slid her eyes sideways towards me. I met her gaze and shrugged.

I've blown it all now, haven't I?

Ursula lifted the magistrate's letter again. She perused it slowly and looked up at Fiona. She tilted her head and smiled. "I've put two and two together. Your surname's Wall, and you come from Hokitika. Would you be Frank Wall's daughter?"

Fiona leant forwards. "I am. D'you know him?"

"Not personally, but he has quite a reputation in racing circles, hasn't he? I remember his horse 'A Bit Rich' came first in the Nelson Cup last year. My husband and I did extremely well from that win."

I blinked rapidly in surprise. Not just because Frank's horse racing hobby might hold us in good stead with this lady, but also at the thought Ursula Bott had found a man willing to be her husband.

Ursula nodded. "All right. I'll accept this magistrate's letter as proof of your relationship."

Fiona gasped and covered her mouth. I didn't dare smile in case Ursula changed her mind. She returned to my application paperwork, picked up a red pen and annotated the pages with several ticks, then opened a drawer, rummaged for a stamp and pounded it in a blank square on the last sheet.

She leant over her desk and stretched out her hand. "Congratulations. Welcome to Aotearoa New Zealand."

I shook it and blinked at Fiona, who gave a wide grin.

Ursula placed my application and the letters into her folder and closed it. She lay her hands flat on the top. "There's one last step before your visa's complete. A formality."

I nodded my head rapidly. "Sure. What do I have to do? Learn the national anthem? Pledge an oath of allegiance?"

Ursula laughed. "No. You don't need to do those until you apply for citizenship."

She opened my application again, turned it around, and pointed at a long paragraph of small print. She tapped her finger twice on the page. "As you'll have read in the accompanying notes, this new visa you've applied for must be granted outside the country. It's not something we can award onshore."

I read the line of text she indicated and looked up. "What do you mean exactly?"

"I mean, in order for your visa to be finalised, you'll have to leave New Zealand."

28. ONE DAY I'LL FLY AWAY

Ursula leant back in her chair.

I furrowed my brow and tilted my head to one side. "I have to leave New Zealand?"

"Yes, your new visa must be affixed in your passport when it's offshore. You have to travel overseas to a country which has a New Zealand embassy, and they'll stick it in for you."

I sat upright. "But the bridging visa you gave me expires in two weeks, at the start of February. It's peak tourist season. How will I find a flight?"

"Sorry. There are several things within my power, but airline schedules are not one of them."

She stood up, pulled her chair back and held the door open.

≈ ≈ ≈

Fiona and I ate lunch at a shopping mall food court, surrounded by young families whose summer holiday enjoyment primarily comprised strolling around fashion stores and stuffing their faces with McDonalds burgers. I leant on my elbows and held my face in my hands.

"Stop looking so despondent," said Fiona. "She said you've qualified for the visa. You can remain in New Zealand for as long as you want."

"I know, I know, you're right. But where shall I have the stamp put in my passport?"

"Why don't you fly back to England and visit your dad? He hasn't seen you for over a year, and isn't it his birthday in February?"

I sat up, beamed and pointed in the air. "What a fantastic idea. I could go home and surprise him. D'you think we can afford it?"

"I reckon so. We've saved a couple of thousand from your music earnings. Why don't you pop into House of Travel and ask about the cost of tickets? There's a branch in this shopping mall somewhere." She gave me a playful grin. "I'll visit the clothes shops. You won't be interested in them, will you?"

≈ ≈ ≈

Photographs of palm-fringed lagoons and butter-coloured beaches covered Fiji and Australia brochures in House of Travel. I idly flicked through their offerings while two agents served clients. A lady addressed the middle-aged ginger-haired man behind the desk, who removed his circular spectacles and cleaned them as she explained her concerns.

"This holiday you've booked for us to explore America; we're celebrating my 60th birthday. I'm sure you sell these tours every day, but we've never travelled outside New Zealand so it's a big adventure."

She deposited her brown handbag on his desk and inspected him over her half-rimmed glasses.

The travel agent smiled genially. "Of course, d'you have any questions?"

"In Orlando, please ensure our room has a proper sea view. My sister booked a hotel on the Gold Coast advertised as having a sea view, and she had to stand on the bed to glimpse the ocean. How ridiculous. Can you telephone the hotel and tell them we must have a view of the sea?"

"I can, but Orlando's not on the coast. I don't think any rooms will have a sea view."

"Of course they will. Look, here, on this map of America." She pointed to the wall beside the agent's desk and tapped Florida twice with her finger. "See? Here's Orlando. It's on the coast. Florida's exceptionally thin."

The travel agent sighed and tapped his keyboard. "I'll request a room with a sea view. In Orlando. Is that all?"

I smiled and covered my mouth. I hoped the lady had a shopping list.

She rotated a piece of paper on the desk and pressed her finger against it. "I don't understand what you've done with our internal flights. After we've left the Grand Canyon, our flight to Las Vegas says it lands five minutes after it takes off. How absurd. You must have made a mistake on the itinerary."

The travel agent looked at the piece of paper. "I see what you mean. Let me check."

He tapped his keyboard and peered at the screen. "No, it's correct. The flight crosses a time zone. You lose an hour during the flight."

"It doesn't cross a time zone. How can it? It's an internal flight."

The travel agent raised his eyebrows. "All right, I'll double check with the airline. Anything else?"

"Yes. My husband's keen to see a bear. Where on our American trip would we have the best chance to observe a wild one, close up?"

The travel agent's mouth formed an evil grin, and he rubbed his hands together. "Now, that, madam, I can definitely assist you with."

"Excuse me, may I help you?"

The other agent distracted me from the conversation about bears, and I relocated to her desk.

"Hello," I said. "I've an urgent request. I need to fly out of the country quickly."

The agent frowned and pursed her lips to one side, and her blonde bob waved as she shrugged and shook her head.

I smiled. "It's all right; I haven't committed any crimes. My working holiday visa expires on February 3rd, and I've been awarded permanent residency."

The agent smiled and sat forwards. "Congratulations."

"Thank you. Unfortunately, my new visa has to be stamped offshore."

"I see. Where were you thinking of heading?"

"I haven't seen my father for over a year, so I wondered if you could book me a flight back to England at the beginning of February. I can visit New Zealand House in London; they can stamp my permanent visa and I'll come back here a few weeks later."

"Hmm. It's the 23rd of January today. The airlines are fully booked with overseas tourists leaving New Zealand after the summer holidays. I'm sure we can find you something, though. What's your budget?"

"As cheap as possible?"

The agent raised her eyebrows. "As cheap as possible in January to England? Okay, I'll see what I can do. Any preference where you stop over?"

"I'd love to see a country I haven't visited before."

She tapped her keyboard. "Air New Zealand via Los Angeles has availability. But we should be able to find something cheaper than $3100."

"Err, yes. I can't afford $3100."

She tapped some more. "Singapore Airlines offer a return flight departing here on January 30th. It's $3000."

"Gosh, these are all rather expensive. I had hoped for something around $1000 less. Plus, I should've mentioned, I can't leave New Zealand until after the 31st. I'm a musician, and I'm playing at an outdoor festival on the West Coast."

"Oh, wow. You mustn't disappoint your fans."

I smiled and glanced down at my lap.

"How about Garuda Indonesia?" she said. "They're well-priced, and there's a seat on February 4th, first thing in the morning. It's $2500."

"I can't leave on the 4th; my visa expires on the 3rd."

"Oh yes, you do have a small window available for travel, don't you?"

The 60-year-old customer who wouldn't make it to 61 without being consumed by a bear had departed, and my agent called over to her colleague. "Brad, any ideas for a return flight to England? I've checked Air New Zealand, Singapore and Garuda."

Brad pushed his chair back and walked over. He leant next to my agent on one hand, and his tie drooped over her keyboard.

She pointed at her screen. "This gentleman has to leave New Zealand between January 31st, when he's playing at a rock concert, and February 3rd, when his visa expires. I'm having trouble finding a reasonably priced flight. The budget's around $2000."

"Peak season ends on the 12th of February, Katie. You won't find anything for $2000 before then. May I sit at your computer?"

They swapped places, and he shoved his sleeves up and cracked his knuckles. "First, we'll keep you in immigration's good books. You have to skedaddle from New Zealand by February the 3rd? Here's what we'll do. Let's hop you across the ditch to Australia."

He tapped the keyboard rapidly.

"Australia?" I said. "I've never been to Australia. I've friends in Brisbane I could stay with."

Brad looked at me and grinned. "An Englishman who's travelled to New Zealand without stopping in Australia? You're a man after my own heart."

Brad rubbed his spectacles again and peered at the screen. "Then, we can fly to England straight from Australia on February the 12th for $1700 return."

I raised my eyebrows and nodded. "Wow. That's much more within my budget."

"Air New Zealand and Virgin have a round-the-world partnership. You can fly from Brisbane to Hong Kong with Air New Zealand, take a Virgin plane to London, and board Air New Zealand again for the return to Christchurch via Los Angeles."

He pressed the enter key triumphantly, like a concert pianist completing a particularly complicated movement. "$1700, plus $299 for the flight to Australia. So, $1999 in total."

He spun the screen around to me and tapped his hand twice on the top. I scanned the lines of orange gibberish.

"Great, where do I sign?"

Brad grinned. "Let's lock it in. How long did you want to spend in Hong Kong?"

"Maybe two days?"

"Shall I reserve you accommodation? The Peninsula Hotel often has a deal."

"No, thanks, I'll find a cheap backpackers."

"Okay. Then Virgin from Hong Kong to London, arriving the morning of the 15th. How many nights will you stay in England?"

"Two weeks. I must be there on February 19th; it's my dad's birthday."

"No problem. D'you want to break the journey in L.A. on the way back to New Zealand?"

"Sure, could I have a couple of nights there? I'll buy some presents for my girlfriend."

"Good move, as you'll have missed Valentine's day." He grinned. "All right, so returning to Christchurch on March the 4th. Sounds good?"

"Perfect. Thanks."

"Great. I've held those for you. Now, the flight to Australia. Air New Zealand flies from Christchurch to Brisbane twice a day."

I shuffled in my seat and sat on my hands. This all seemed to be proceeding remarkably well.

Brad tapped his computer, inspected his screen and furrowed his brow. "February 1st, 2nd and 3rd are full. There's one seat on the evening flight on the 31st. Is it that day you're playing at a rock concert?

"Yes, it's an afternoon thing. What time's the flight?"

"10.05 p.m."

Brad glanced up and down his screen. "In fact, that's the only flight with availability the entire week."

I shrugged. "I don't seem to have a choice."

≈ ≈ ≈

Fiona had invested her time fondling thousands of garments in a shop called Glassons.

I observed her empty arms. "Have you actually bought anything?"

"I tried on a jumper, but I changed my mind. I might still get it."

She picked up a dress and held it against her. "What d'you think?"

"Lovely. You should buy it."

Fiona rotated it and caressed it some more. "I'm not sure it's me."

She hung up the dress. "How d'you go at the House of Travel?"

"Great. I'll give you all the details when you've finished shopping."

"I've finished shopping."

She plucked a skirt off a hanger. I tapped my foot and twiddled my thumbs.

Fiona replaced the skirt. "Come on. Tell me on the drive back to Hokitika."

≈ ≈ ≈

The flat checkerboard of the Canterbury Plains stretched out towards the Alps, as the suburbs of Christchurch vanished behind us. The snow had departed from the summits, and fluffy cotton clouds drifted past the peaks. I fidgeted in the passenger seat as Fiona stepped through a lengthy conversation about a school friend of hers she'd encountered in the shopping mall.

"D'you know, she's 22, and she's had two children already, and another on the way. I've no idea how she's going to cope with three kids under four years old. And I don't suppose her boyfriend'll help; he spends his time hunting deer with his mates. Mind you, her mother had her at nineteen. I can't think why anyone would want to be tied down at that age. I'd love to have kids, but later on, you know?"

"Yes."

"Anyway, I told her we'd have to meet up next time I'm in Christchurch. I suppose I should buy something for the new baby. I reckon she won't be short of hand-me-downs."

I let out a loud breath. "So, d'you want to hear what happened at House of Travel?"

"Oh, yes. Of course."

"Right. Well, I'm going on a world tour."

"Wow. I wish I could come with you. Where d'you start?"

"I fly out of Christchurch on the 31st of January."

"Hang on, that's the day of the agricultural and pastoral show."

"I know, but the flight's not until the evening."

Fiona glanced at me, gripped the wheel again and accelerated around a corner.

"My first stop's Brisbane," I said.

"Brisbane? I thought you were flying to England."

"I am, eventually. I had to leave New Zealand before my visa expired, and the best way to do it at a price we could afford was to hop over to Brisbane."

"Okay, how long are you in Australia?"

"About ten days. I'll stay with my friends I met backpacking through Europe. I can't wait. It'll be great to be travelling again."

"Right, then where?"

"Then I board a plane to Hong Kong, stop there for two nights, and connect to Virgin for the flight to London."

Fiona tapped her fingers on the steering wheel. "I've heard the shopping's amazing in Hong Kong. And there's fabulous night markets. I'm so envious."

"I promise I'll take you to Hong Kong one day; I'll take photos. Anyway, I'm staying two weeks in London with Dad; I'll drop by our flat to ensure it's still there, visit a few friends, and go to New Zealand House so they can stamp my visa."

"Your trip sounds so exciting. Will you be doing much shopping in London? Oxford Street, or Brent Cross? Or Camden Market? I love Camden Market."

"Umm, I've no plans to, but on the way back, I'm spending a couple of nights in Los Angeles." I winked. "I'll shop for you at Fashion Valley."

Fiona glared at me. "Oh my goodness, I'm so jealous. I wish we had enough money so I could travel with you. I loved Fashion Valley when we stopped on our way to Tonga. We were there for an afternoon; I could've spent a week."

She pursed her lips to one side and ran her hand through her hair. "All this talk about Hong Kong, and London, and Los Angeles; I loved life in our little flat in London; I'd do anything to live there again. Can we make that happen?"

29. FAME

I placed my right hand on her leg.

"Please, let's talk about the next stage of our lives once I return from overseas. At least once my New Zealand permanent residency's been finalised we'll be able to stay in the same country forever if we want to."

Fiona placed her hand on top of mine and squeezed it. "I'll miss you. We've never been apart for a month before."

"It'll pass quickly. I'll be back before you know it."

"It'll pass significantly quicker for you, swanning around the globe while I'm stuck here."

I gazed at the red-flowered trees pouring down the mountains. "Could we stop in Arthur's Pass Village? I need a pee."

≈ ≈ ≈

I shook Frank and Phillip's hands, hugged Linda and said goodbye to my home on the farm. Jazz rubbed his nose against my leg, and I crouched and buried my face in his thick, brown fur.

"It's not farewell for ever," said Linda. "You'll return in four weeks with your shiny new permanent visa, and then you can live here for the rest of your life."

Frank grinned. "Well, won't that be wonderful?"

Fiona pressed her lips together. "Dad'll drop me at the A & P show later and I'll drive you to Christchurch airport. Enjoy the day."

I rattled my car keys. "I can't be late for my big stadium performance. Frank, how will I find Athol Olsen?"

"Look out for a guy with a brimmed, leather hat. You can't miss him."

"All right, thanks."

I turned the ignition, accelerated along the gravel drive and waved from the driver's window, as a cloud of dust obscured the family.

≈ ≈ ≈

A man in a Massey Ferguson baseball cap gesticulated at me as I drove through the show grounds.

He can't be Athol Olsen. Frank said a leather hat.

I wound down my window.

The man pointed. "You can't drive through this way. The car park's behind you."

"I'm the entertainer for the afternoon. The band. I need to park as close to the stage as possible."

"If you're an exhibitor, you should have an E pass in your windscreen."

"I don't have an E pass; could I unload at the stage and park elsewhere? The gear weighs a ton."

I pointed with my thumb at my amplifier and speakers in the back of the car. He bent down and inspected them.

"All right." He moved a barrier. "Head for the open-sided truck. When you've finished, pop your car in the main car park."

"Thanks. Also, could you tell me where to find Athol Olsen?"

"I saw him a minute ago. He wears a brimmed, leather hat; you can't miss him."

"Okay, thank you." I switched on my hazard lights and trundled forwards.

≈ ≈ ≈

Directly in front of the open-sided truck trailer that formed the stage, a circular grass area had been fenced off.

This must be for my fans. The mosh pit.

Beyond this lawn, horse boxes and farm trucks surrounded the Hokitika racetrack. Cows, sheep and pigs stood inside metal-railed pens, and dog-owners towed their canines around on leads. White ropes denoted a display area, and tiny children with yellow jodhpurs and black riding hats mounted German Shepherd-sized ponies.

A Travel Adventure in Search of New Zealand Rock Stardom

A Ferris wheel towered above the action, and toddlers spun on a small merry-go-round while a procession of people carried baskets of vegetables and cakes into a hall.

I liked this scene. A celebration of country life. And my own version of *Live Aid*. I dragged my equipment up the three steps, put my hands on my hips, smiled and unpacked. An extension lead poked out of the rear of the stage, so I plugged in my gear, and a switch illuminated on my amplifier.

Phew. At least there's power.

I stood in front of my microphone, connected my tuner, plucked each string and adjusted the guitar's machine heads. I recalled Cage preparing The Gear Junkies' equipment in Christchurch, crossed my fingers, and hoped my performance today would run as smoothly. The microphone switch was set to 'off', so I touched my lips to it and murmured, "Hello, Wembley. I'm London Musician Simon Michael Prior, and this is *Live Aid*."

Someone tapped my shoulder. I felt my cheeks tingle, and I turned around slowly. A leather hat with a round-faced, checked-shirted man beneath it nodded at me.

"Simon?"

The hat brandished a black clipboard in one hand and a fat, multi-coloured ball-point pen in the other.

"I'm Simon. Would you be Athol Olsen?"

"I am." He shook my hand. "Thanks for coming today. It'll be great to have music between the exhibits. If this works out, we might do it every year." He flipped a page over on his clipboard and ticked the word 'guitarist'.

"No problem, Athol; thanks for asking me. I'm so excited about this afternoon's concert."

Athol leant towards me so his hat brim bonked my shoulder. "D'you know a man called Dennis Stark?"

Bloody hell. Has he sabotaged this event as well?

"I'm aware of him, yes."

"He was sniffing around earlier. He said I shouldn't have employed you 'cos you're crap. According to him, I ought to have booked some other bloke he knows from Christchurch."

"Right, and how did you respond?"

"I told him, you do things your way, Dennis, and I'll run my show my way. I'll book who I want, thank you very much."

215

I grinned. I reckoned I was going to get along with Athol Olsen very well indeed.

He lay his clipboard on one of my speakers. "Here's the order of events; I'll leave you a copy." He ran his finger down the list. "This morning there's the horse judging, the cattle judging and the sheep judging, which all happen on the field over there."

He waved his arm in the direction of the racetrack. I glanced up at a line of white gazebos, which reminded me of a medieval military encampment.

"Then there's the small pet competition and the axe-men demonstrating the wood chopping." He rotated his wrist, glanced at his watch and scribbled on his sheet.

"At twelve noon, the president will open the show. He might want to use your microphone. Will that be okay?"

"Of course."

"Once he's finished, if you could begin some background music before the guide dog display on the grass in front of the stage at 12.30."

He indicated the fenced off lawn. "At one o'clock the Kokatahi Band'll play."

I furrowed my brow and tilted my head. "Kokatahi Band? I thought you didn't have bands?"

"They're not a band like you; it's folk music. They play various unusual instruments: banjos, penny whistles and shakers. Incredible old boys. And a few ladies."

"Oh, wow. I look forward to hearing them. I love watching any music played with skill."

"After they finish, it's the Boys Brigade' at 1.30, and you're on again at two."

This all seems well organised.

"Sure."

"The next part's a demonstration by the volunteer firefighters, followed by the guide dogs' second outing."

"Gosh, it's a full afternoon."

"Yep, a lot to cram in a short space of time."

Athol flipped his page over. "At 3.15, we'll have the Grand Parade, and finally, if you wrap up the show at 3.30 that'd be great."

Plenty of time to perform a massive finale before my flight.

"Sounds fine, Athol."

≈ ≈ ≈

I ambled over to the racetrack to watch the sheep judging. Children of various ages pulled off-white lambs around in a circle. The lambs weren't used to being attached to string and didn't understand the concept of circles. I smiled at a boy untangling his lamb's tow-rope from his ankles.

A man in a blazer and Panama hat held a megaphone. "In second place, Scott Byers, showing Lucy."

The audience applauded as a young boy with ginger hair stepped forward, tugging a lamb which didn't want to be tugged. He accepted a certificate, turned around and grinned.

The compère continued. "And first prize in the children's lamb category goes to Jill Waters, showing Dolly."

The crowd clapped louder. A girl in a faded pink dress dragged her lamb towards the judge, who presented her with a small, plastic trophy as Dolly lifted her tail and presented her own small trophy on the grass behind her.

"Congratulations, Jill," said the announcer. "The next category will be the lead rein ponies…"

I wandered away and found a caravan selling coffee.

11.15.

Ages until my star turn.

A man positioned logs of wood between supports. He noticed me watching him.

"G'day, mate. Are you here for the wood chopping?"

I laughed. "No chance. I'm not sure I've ever swung an axe in my life, apart from my guitar. I'm this afternoon's musician, Simon Michael Prior."

"Roger Mansell. Pleased to meet you." He held out a hand attached to a Popeye-sized forearm.

"Athol mentioned he'd booked a band. What sort of music d'you perform?"

"A bit of everything. The '60s to the '90s. I suppose I should play some country and western, as this is an agricultural and pastoral show."

He gazed at the crowd milling around the animals and the tents. "I reckon you could play anything; these people have consumed a few drinks already. And it's not even lunchtime."

≈ ≈ ≈

I finished my coffee and pushed through the crowds. People applauded, as a flat-capped man stepped forward and accepted a rosette and a silver trophy. The audience dispersed towards the food caravans, and I climbed the three steps to the stage.

Stage.

My stage.

My *Live Aid*.

I slung my guitar around my neck, played a few silent test chords and reviewed my song list. A group of people glanced in my direction, and I waved and acknowledged them.

11.55.

Five minutes.

Five minutes until the president opened the event.

Then—showtime.

≈ ≈ ≈

A tall, thin, bald man dressed in a blue blazer and brown slacks held onto the handrail and pulled himself up the steps. Athol followed him.

"Mr Bradshaw, meet Simon, who's playing music for us today. Simon, this is Ernest Bradshaw, the president."

I shook his hand as Athol retreated down the stairs. Ernest extracted a sheaf of paper from the inside pocket of his blazer, stooped to my microphone and tapped it.

"Is this microscope working, Simon?"

"Yes, Mr Bradshaw. The, erm, microscope is working."

Ernest addressed the throng. "Good afternoon, ladies and gentlemen, boys and girls."

"Stand closer," I said. "They'll hear you better."

His lips brushed against the microphone's head, and I made a mental note to wipe it before I sang anything.

"Good afternoon, ladies and gentlemen, boys and girls."

His voice echoed through my speakers. I stood to one side and watched the crowd swivel in our direction.

Ernest continued. "May I welcome you all to the 28th annual Westland Agricultural and Pastoral show here in our wonderful little town of Hokitika."

He paused, and the crowd applauded. I wiped sweat onto my jeans.

Wow.

This is real.

"I'm sure you've all enjoyed watching the animal judging and the various sideshows. I used to be a bit of a wood-chopper myself in my youth."

Polite laughter.

"May I thank Athol Olsen and his wonderful team of volunteers for all their organisation, preparing for the day, setting up the show and making sure everything runs smoothly."

Applause.

I gazed across the sea of heads to find Athol's hat, but he'd disappeared to organise someone.

"And also, I'd like to thank the Westland Racing Club for allowing us once more to hold our event at the Hokitika Racecourse."

More applause.

"Now, without further ado, may I declare the 1998 Westland Agricultural and Pastoral show open, and to kick off proceedings..," he pulled his glasses down his nose and examined his notes, "..London Musician: Simon Michael Prior."

I cracked my knuckles, faced the microphone and froze.

30. THE SHOW MUST GO ON

My pulse raced, and adrenaline tingled through my body.
This is it.
The pinnacle of my musical career.
I'm not a pommy busker, I'm Brian May.
And this is my Live Aid.

"Helloooo Hokitika." I thrust one clenched fist erect in the air. I'd seen Bob Geldof do this, so I reckoned this must be the correct gesture for the occasion.

Athol Olsen glanced at me as he marched past on his way to co-ordinate upcoming spectacles.

I took a deep breath. "I'm London Musician Simon Michael Prior, and I'll be entertaining you until the end of this wonderful Westland Agricultural and Pastoral show today."

My potential fans chatted and drank out of cans and glasses and looked everywhere except in the direction of the stage.

Here we go.

I started the riff to 'Lyin' Eyes'. A relaxed, country song for a relaxed, country show.

People strolled past in the sunshine.

'I Only Want to Be with You' segued into 'Take Me Home, Country Roads'.

Queues formed for the merry-go-round and ferris wheel.

'Proud Mary' and 'Mr. Tambourine Man' sounded from my speakers.

Children carried balloons. Mothers carried children. Fathers carried beers.

Bloody hell. I'm not supposed to be background music. Maybe I should blast some more upbeat numbers.

I performed 'Live It Up'.
Nobody lived it up.
I played 'Wild Thing'.
Nobody went wild.

'I'm a Believer' showed there weren't any believers in today's crowd.

Athol ascended the steps and mouthed at me.

Guy togs?

I sang another verse. He waved his arms, stabbed his clipboard so hard I expected his finger to perforate it and pointed to the edge of the field. His mouth worked overtime.

Guide dogs. Got it.

"And now," I announced, "please clear the lawn for the guide dog display."

My first set as a live stadium performer was over. I stuffed my hands in my pockets and sighed.

Live Aid, where are you?

Athol scuttled off to organise something else as I chugged from a bottle of water and glanced at the dog handlers assembling an obstacle course. Three Labrador retrievers waited with a lady. I stepped down from the stage and wandered amongst the crowd.

Doesn't anyone recognise me?

Doesn't anyone want my autograph?

I'm the rock star, for goodness' sake.

≈ ≈ ≈

Athol Olsen's hat sprinted around the edge of the arena. He gesticulated, glanced at his watch and waved his clipboard. I watched a simulation of a guide dog helping a blind man negotiate a set of steps and concluded Athol's tight itinerary was seriously under threat.

"How's it going, Athol?" I asked.

"Not well. The guide dogs took so long to set up, we're at least thirty minutes behind schedule. They'll have to break down while the Kokatahi Band's playing."

He waved his clipboard at a man in a red-and-white band member's uniform. "Joe, can you start now? The guide dogs are finishing, but we're late."

He flicked over a page of notes and looked around. "Where's the Boys' Brigade?"

I pointed helpfully at another man wearing a blue outfit with a white diagonal sash.

"Yep, Chris is there, but where's the kids?" He waved and shouted. "Where's the boys, Chris?"

"They're buying ice creams. Are you ready for us?"

Athol tapped his watch. "Ten minutes, Chris. Ten minutes. And can you shorten your demonstration? We're running behind."

I watched his hat beetle away, as the Kokatahi Band began a tune I recognised from my primary school days as 'Head, Shoulders, Knees and Toes'.

Chris blew a whistle; the guide dogs exited the arena and the boys' brigade formed two teams. They assembled complicated contraptions using garden canes and elastic bands, then Chris whistled again. The teams screwed up sheets of newspaper, placed them in the constructions and fired them at each other. The crowd clapped and yelled encouragement as the homemade catapults landed direct hits on the opposition. I grinned at their antics. Athol materialised beside me and tapped his wrist.

"Time to restart. A couple of quick songs while I find the firefighters. I'm not allowing the guide dogs to have their second turn. We're too far behind schedule. Bloody hell."

The boys brigade bowed, and I leapt on stage like an Olympic hurdler.

"What a fantastic display, ladies and gentlemen, boys and girls. Stick around for more acts, meanwhile, here's Dire Straits, and 'Walk of Life'."

Several people watched me from the edge of the field. One woman clapped, and another waved her hands in the air. A third lady grabbed their arms, and the trio gyrated. Other people shouted and encouraged them.

Three ladies wiggling in the aisle doth not a Live Aid make.

"Anyone else for a boogie?" I called, as in a desperate attempt to increase the atmosphere, I merged 'Walk of Life' into 'Jessie's Girl'.

Come on, please dance. Please.

Athol Olsen wrote on his clipboard and nodded at me. I couldn't work out what his head movement meant, so I followed 'Honky Tonk Women' with 'Stuck in the Middle with You'. Athol sliced his hand backwards and forwards across his throat like a gruesome scene from *The Krays* as men and women sprinted onto the lawn carrying ladders.

Stealers Wheel truncated mid-chorus, and I lay my guitar in its stand and stepped down from the stage with my hands in my pockets.

This stadium experience isn't exactly how I imagined.

≈ ≈ ≈

"Hello, how are you getting on?"

"Hi, Fiona."

I shrugged one shoulder.

"What's wrong?" she asked.

"My performance isn't the big event I hoped it would be. Hardly anyone's watching me or dancing. This isn't exactly bloody *Live Aid*, is it?"

"You might need to reduce your expectations."

I lowered my voice. "Between you and me, I should've continued playing. These guide dogs and Morris men won't hold the crowd's attention."

"Far out; this event isn't all about you. These people haven't come especially to see London Musician Simon Michael Prior. We're celebrating the country community: the farmers, the animals, the children's activities. And don't call the Kokatahi Band Morris men. They've been performing since my grandad's childhood."

My cheeks reddened, and I clasped my hands in front of me.

She tugged a twenty dollar note from her jeans pocket. "Come on, misery guts. D'you want to grab a bite?"

"Okay, sure. I can make time before the next set. Hopefully, more people show some interest."

Fiona led me to a food caravan. She picked up a burger and some chips, and we sat at a wooden trestle table.

She held my arm. "I can't believe you're boarding a plane tonight, and we'll be separated for a month. We've hardly been apart one night for the last two years. Which part of your travels are you most excited about?"

"Hong Kong, I reckon; I've always wanted to visit. It seems so exotic. So...foreign. And Australia of course. I spent oodles of time at university gawping at Kylie Minogue in *Neighbours* when I should've been studying. I'd love to see where it's filmed."

She unwrapped her burger and bit a semi-circle from it. "*Neighbours* is shot in Melbourne. You're going to Brisbane."

I picked up a chip and brandished it to show I'd won the unwritten competition to discover the biggest. "I could drive to Melbourne and visit the set?"

"Sure. It'll only take you a week to travel there and back."

"Gosh. Australia's so big. It makes the distances in New Zealand seem tiny."

Fiona smiled and shook her head. "I bet you can't wait to see your dad again."

"I'll take him out for his birthday to his favourite restaurant in Chinatown. And to the theatre. I'll see what's showing in Leicester Square."

Fiona gazed towards the mountains and sighed. "I'm so envious. I miss the culture in London so much. D'you think we'll live there again?"

I held her hand. "Please, let's leave this discussion until I return from England?"

"I hope I can hold out that long."

I twisted her wrist to see her watch. "Time to prepare for my next set. Are you staying at the show?"

"Yep. Dad's toddled off to the betting shop. I'll be here for the afternoon. When d'you go back on?"

"I close the show at 3.30 after the Grand Parade. Plenty of time to drive to the airport."

"Wow, you're the last act? That's incredible."

"Could you bring the car around at four p.m? It's in the main car park."

I handed her the keys. "Drive as close to the stage as possible. I'll need to load up immediately if we're going to reach the airport on time."

"Okay. Four o'clock. No problem."

She swallowed the last piece of pattie, finished her chips and dumped the rubbish in a bin.

≈ ≈ ≈

I took a deep breath as the Grand Parade dissipated. The entire congregation of spectators assembled in front of the stage as if they expected Freddie Mercury himself to prance on stage.

This is it, Simon.
Your final, live, stadium set.
Keep the audience. They're ready and waiting for you.

"What a fantastic show we've had, ladies and gentlemen; I hope you've all enjoyed the day's activities. And now, let your hair down to some Neil Diamond."

I planted my feet wide and sang as loud as I could. The crowd jiggled and clapped. A few of them clapped in time. Four ladies wearing summer dresses choreographed a dance routine, as less-willing participants melted into the background. More women joined them, and a crowd gyrating to 'Sweet Caroline' covered the arena. Men stood at the edge of the grass and held their partners' drinks.

Yes!
This is my show.
This is what I was born to do.

Several thousand people applauded and cheered as the song finished.

Need to keep momentum. Here we go. 'Summer of '69'.

I struck the first chords of the Bryan Adams classic. Ladies dragged less-willing men onto the grass and the atmosphere escalated several notches. I gazed across the sea of faces and grinned so wide it hurt. Two blonde girls in bikini tops sat on their partner's shoulders and waved hands in the air.

Yes! Yes! Yes! This is like Live Aid.

I'd never seen so many people all focussed on me. 'Summer of '69' merged into 'Born to Be Wild'. A choir of thousands yelled the chorus. I raised one fist above my head in a celebratory salute, glanced left and met eyes with Dennis Stark.

31. LEAVING ON A JET PLANE

Dennis Stark stood alone at the perimeter of the crowd, shovelling his hand into a bucket of popcorn. He glared at me, shook his head, dropped his litter on the ground and walked away. I watched his retreating back then returned my gaze to more important matters.

My crowd.

My audience.

My fans.

I couldn't risk 'Living Next Door to Alice' so I launched into 'Mustang Sally'. At the appropriate point in the chorus, several thousand voices joined in the refrain. A tingle spread outwards from my body, and goosebumps broke out all over my arms.

I played 'Twist and Shout'. Summer dresses spun, and cowboy boots jived like a scene from *Footloose*. I stepped forwards during an instrumental and peeked around the side of the stage.

Where's Fiona?

My mind pendulumed between the thrill of entertaining the crowd and the agony of departing for the airport on time. I bit my lip and glanced at my song list.

Shit. What's next? I'd only planned five songs in this set. 'Johnny B. Goode'. Here we go.

The audience clapped and cheered at the opening riff. Hundreds of air guitars swung simultaneously.

This is the best feeling I've ever had, but it must be at least 4.15. Where the hell's Fiona? We have to leave.

I wanted to stop playing, but I didn't want to stop playing. I might never have this opportunity again. 'Zombie' by The Cranberries. 'Jack & Diane' by John Cougar. 'Tubthumping' by Chumbawamba.

Right up to date.

The entire audience performed a routine where they crouched down and jumped up again repeatedly. Some of them executed these moves in time with the music. My jaw ached from grinning.

I had the crowd in my hand.

My stadium gig.

My *Live Aid*.

I ran my hands back through my hair and played 'Summer of '69' again.

≈ ≈ ≈

It must be 4.30. I have to finish. This is crazy; Fiona can't be lost.

"Thank you very much; you've been a great crowd. I'll see you next time."

Thousands applauded. One woman at the front cried out, "more, more."

I bowed, waved, dumped my guitar in its case, clicked off several power buttons and unplugged cables. The applause died down, and the audience dispersed.

A young lady with straight, blonde hair approached the stage. "You're not finishing, are you? We're just getting fired up."

"Sorry, I have to. I'm headed to London this evening."

"Oh wow, did they fly you in from England for this show?"

I laughed. "No, I live in Hokitika. I'm returning for a visit. I'll be back in a few weeks."

Where are you, Fiona?

The blonde girl tossed her hair over her shoulder and fiddled with her gold necklace. "D'you have a business card? I might book you for my 21st."

"Yep, I do. One sec."

I fished in my guitar case. "Here. Sorry, I must keep going; I'm in a hurry."

I coiled cables around my lower arm and stuffed them in a bag.

She turned the card over and back again, smiled, and stroked her lower lip. "Excuse me, Simon. It doesn't say on your card whether you're single?"

My cheeks flushed, as I heard a voice behind me say, "He's not."

I turned around and threw my hands in the air. "Where the hell have you been, Fiona? It's after four-thirty. I'm going to miss the bloody flight."

"Calm down. We'll be at the airport on time; it's going to be okay."

The blonde lady folded her arms and sauntered away.

I shook my palms either side of my head and yelled. "It's not going to be okay; you'll have to drive like a bloody maniac over the pass to make up time. Why are you so late?"

"Don't be angry with me, or I'll tell that girl you are single."

My shoulders slumped. "Sorry, sorry. But seriously, how come you weren't here at four?"

"They wouldn't allow me into the exhibitors' area. They wanted an E pass, which I didn't have, so I couldn't drive through the barrier until the show finished."

I shook my head, stuffed my guitar in its case and clicked it shut.

"Anyway," said Fiona. "Relax. I rang Air New Zealand from the phone box, and the flight's delayed. We'll make it."

A slow smile decorated my face, and I hugged her. I combed my hand back through my hair, swivelled, and surveyed the scene.

Scattered groups chatted and finished drinks.

Men and women dismantled gazebos and packed away chairs and tables.

A man wearing a bright yellow vest dragged a black rubbish sack around the lawn. He collected empty bottles and food wrappers with a long grabbing tool.

I puffed out my cheeks and flattened my hands on my head.

Has this all been a dream?

Did I really just perform a stadium gig?

Did I really play to a crowd of thousands?

I shoved the guitar and speakers into the car, Fiona started the engine, and we bumped across the field towards the exit. I lay in the passenger seat, closed my eyes and tipped my head back, as tension released from my body.

I'd done it.

I'd performed at a big outdoor event.

I'd had the crowd in my hand.

I'd played my *Live Aid*.

"Penny for your thoughts?" said Fiona.

The relentless Tasman breakers smashed on the shoreline. Heat haze shimmered to my right, as fifty shades of green trees stretched up towards the Southern Alps.

"I'm thinking about how I'll miss life with you on the West Coast. It'll feel strange, being in big cities again after a year here in the country."

I reached across the gear stick and squeezed her leg.

For the first time, I'd be travelling without her.

Without my girlfriend.

Without my constant companion.

Alone.

I released her thigh. She changed gear, and we accelerated towards the mountains.

EPILOGUE

Thank you very much for reading the third in my *South Pacific Shenanigans* series.

Hokitika rightly promotes itself as a 'Cool Little Town' and if you're in the South Island of New Zealand, I strongly recommend you spend a couple of days there. The mountains, lakes, rivers and forests are breathtaking, and there are activities for everyone. Why not check out https://hokitika.org/ and plan a visit?

Tane, the landlord of the Minersville Tavern, continued to refuse to pay me despite the court order. The tribunal fined him for non-payment, and he ended up spending significantly more money than if he'd paid me correctly in the first place. Pania has clearly been forgiven for sticking up for me as she still works at the pub.

Athol Olsen organises the Westland Agricultural and Pastoral show as enthusiastically as ever. He also plays with the Kokatahi band, and continues to wear his brimmed, leather hat.

Mike Keenan retired from being Westland council events manager and spends his days driving tourists around the West Coast and telling lengthy and complicated Irish jokes.

D'you remember Ian Prior, who introduced himself after I'd played at Tom Newell's party? During my research for this book, I looked him up and discovered he has a Wikipedia page. You can read about him here: https://en.wikipedia.org/wiki/Ian_Prior_(doctor). Sadly, I never took up his offer to visit him in Wellington; I wish I had.

I never discovered the real reason why Fiona's teacher retired. That'll have to remain a mystery to all of us.

And what happened next to Fiona and me? Well, we've had plenty of adventures, and you'll be able to read about more of them in the next *South Pacific Shenanigans* book, due to be published in 2023. While you're waiting, feel free to check out other books in the series. Links to them are on the following pages.

A Travel Adventure in Search of New Zealand Rock Stardom

PLEASE REVIEW THE POMEGRANATE BUSKER

If you enjoyed *The Pomegranate Busker*, please consider leaving a review, to let other readers know.

I've made it super-easy for you; all you have to do is browse to the link below or scan the QR code and it'll take you straight to the right page.

Thanks so much, it means a lot to me.

Simon

Smarturl.it/pomegranatereview

SOUTH PACIFIC SHENANIGANS

What happens next to Simon and Fiona?

Will Simon successfully circumnavigate the world without Fiona, and return safely to New Zealand?

Will Fiona come to terms with life on the West Coast, or will the pull to bright city lights prove too much for her?

Find out, in the upcoming fourth book in the *South Pacific Shenanigans* series.

To be the first to find out about its release, and to see what Simon and Fiona are up to now, sign up for Simon's monthly newsletter at:

simonmichaelprior.com

A Travel Adventure in Search of New Zealand Rock Stardom

PHOTOS TO ACCOMPANY THE POMEGRANATE BUSKER

If you'd like to see photos that accompany *The Pomegranate Busker*, including unused promotional photos and images of a baby cow being born, please head over to my website or scan the QR code and click the book's cover.

simonmichaelprior.com

MUSIC TO ACCOMPANY THE POMEGRANATE BUSKER

If you'd like to listen to the music that Simon played in his pub, party and festival gigs as described in *The Pomegranate Busker*, please visit the link or scan the QR code to hear it on Spotify:

smarturl.it/pomegranateplaylist

A Travel Adventure in Search of New Zealand Rock Stardom

DISCLAIMER

This is a work in the genre creative non-fiction. I have tried to recreate events, locales and conversations from my memories of them. To maintain their anonymity, in some instances I have changed the names of individuals and places. Some characters in this book are composites, comprised of more than one person I met. I may have changed some identifying characteristics and details such as physical properties, occupations and places of residence. Any mistakes are all my own work. SMP.

BOOK 1 IN THE SERIES: THE COCONUT WIRELESS

When Simon and Fiona embark on a quest to track down the Queen of Tonga, they have no idea they'll end up marooned on a desert island.

No idea they'll encounter an undiscovered tribe, rescue a drowning actress, learn jungle survival from a commando, and attend cultural ceremonies few Westerners have seen.

As they find out who hooks up, who breaks up, who cracks up, and who throws up, will they fulfil Simon's ambition to see the queen, or will they be distracted by insomniac chickens, grunting wild piglets, and the easy-going Tongan lifestyle?

Read the first few chapters FREE by visiting the link, or scanning the QR code:

Smarturl.it/lookinsidecoconut

A Travel Adventure in Search of New Zealand Rock Stardom

BOOK 2 IN THE SERIES:
THE SCENICLAND RADIO

When English city boy Simon follows his girlfriend across the world to her family farm in remotest New Zealand, he has no idea he'll be force-fed a meal of beetle larva, get pushed off the road by half a house, and be inspected by indignant penguins and flattened by a giant leaf-blower.

As he poisons the milk, dive-bombs the bulls, and loses the herd of cows in a river, will he ever learn to be a farmer, or will he have to stop impersonating a country boy, and return to London?

Read the first few chapters FREE by visiting the link, or scanning the QR code:

Smarturl.it/lookinsidescenicland

A Travel Adventure in Search of New Zealand Rock Stardom

ALSO BY SIMON: AN ENGLISHMAN IN NEW YORK

Have you ever wanted a first-hand glimpse into post-war 1940s New York?

When 21-year-old John Miskin Prior travelled by ship to New York in 1948, he had no idea he was going to meet and dine with the Roosevelts and the Rockefellers. No idea he would be among the first ever to see 'South Pacific' and 'Death of a Salesman'. No idea he would witness Truman's election victory, so unexpected, the newspapers were reprinted.

This eyewitness account of an English student living in New York for the incredible year of 1948 – 49 has been collated from his letters discovered after his death, and forms a unique account of the period.

Read the first few chapters FREE by visiting the link, or scanning the QR code:

Smarturl.it/lookinsideenglishman

A Travel Adventure in Search of New Zealand Rock Stardom

ABOUT THE AUTHOR

Simon Michael Prior insists on inflicting all aspects of life on himself so that his readers can enjoy learning about his latest trip / experience / disaster / emotional breakdown (insert phrase of your choice).

During his extended adolescence, now over forty years long, he has lived on two boats and sunk one of them; sold houses, street signs, Indian food and paper bags for a living; visited almost fifty countries and lived in three; qualified as a scuba divemaster; nearly killed himself learning to wakeboard; trained as a search and rescue skipper with the Coast Guard, and built his own house without the benefit of an instruction manual.

Simon is as amazed as anyone that the house is still standing, and he now lives in it by the sea with his wife and twin daughters, where he spends his time regurgitating his experiences on paper before he has so many more that he forgets them.

Website: **simonmichaelprior.com**

Email: **simon@simonmichaelprior.com**

Facebook: **@simonmichaelprior**

Instagram: **@simonmichaelprior**

Twitter: **@simonmichaelpri**

If you would like to receive a regular newsletter about Simon and his writing, and be the first to find out about new releases, please sign up to his mailing list here:

simonmichaelprior.com

ACKNOWLEDGEMENTS

A big thank you to Victoria Twead and all the members of the Facebook group 'We Love Memoirs', for befriending me, encouraging me, educating me, reassuring me, and driving me forward.

This book wouldn't have been possible without the help of the following people: Linda Wall, for helping me fill in details, when my memory failed me. The book's wonderful team of beta readers: Alyson Sheldrake, Alison Ripley-Cubitt, Anna Rashbrook, Judith Benson, Julie Haigh, Liesbet Collaert, Lisa Rose Wright and Pauline Armstrong; your feedback improved the final result so much.

Thank you to Victoria Twead, Meg LaTorre, David Gaughran and Dave Chesson for informative courses, tips and useful tools.

Thank you to Tim Barton, for being a great inspiration and unwittingly allowing me to borrow your entire set.

Thank you to every publican, festival and party organiser on the West Coast who employed me; the journey was educational and enjoyable.

Thank you to Floss and Dave for being my biggest fans, I knew I could always count on you and your support humbled me.

Thank you to Jeff Bezos, for giving independent authors a platform on which to publish our writing.

And thank you so much to Fiona, I couldn't have done it without you.

WE LOVE MEMOIRS

www.ingramcontent.com/pod-product-compliance
Lightning Source LLC
Chambersburg PA
CBHW031241290426
44109CB00012B/392